TAX LOOPHOLES
The legend and the reality

Roger A. Freeman

American Enterprise Institute for Public Policy Research
Washington, D. C.

Hoover Institution on War, Revolution and Peace
Stanford University, Stanford, California

AEI-Hoover Policy Study 5, May 1973
(Hoover Institution Studies 40)

ISBN 08447-3102-1
Library of Congress Catalog Card No. L.C. 73-82205

74-5588

Second printing, April 1974

Printed in United States of America

TAX LOOPHOLES

AEI-Hoover
policy studies

Contents

1
Why Half of All Income Is Not Taxed

Introduction

Leadership pronouncements in both houses of Congress during 1972 make it clear that income tax reform will be a major goal of legislative efforts in 1973. Final action, however, may fall far short of announced aims and could be much less significant and extensive than in the Tax Reform Act of 1969. Yet, the importance of the way in which the tax burden is distributed cannot be overrated at a time when governmental revenues—federal, state and local—equal about 40 percent of total personal income. The load should not only be equitable among economic groups and individuals but also have the least harmful effect on economic growth and stability.

All-encompassing as the term "income tax reform" sounds, it has in recent years come to acquire a more specific connotation—namely, a broadening of the federal tax base by repealing or narrowing remedial provisions that now protect large amounts of personal income from taxation, or at least from the full impact of the tax rate schedule. In common terms, reform aims at closing so-called "loopholes" through which it is said much income escapes bearing its proper share of the overall tax burden.

Repeated attempts at reform over the past 15 years have not eliminated the most frequently cited "loopholes." As a result, the chairman of the House Ways and Means Committee, Representative Wilbur Mills, adopted a novel strategy in May 1972: he introduced a bill (H.R. 15230) which called for the repeal, over the next three years, of 54 provisions in existing law that are often referred to as "loopholes." Senate majority leader Mike Mansfield submitted a companion measure (S. 3657) in the Senate. The intent of the bills' sponsors was not to have all or even most of those provisions permanently wiped off the books, but to order them repealed effective in the future—in 1974, 1975 and 1976—so as to force congressional consideration of each provision lest the wholesale repeals go into effect. Representative Mills did not expect Congress to act on tax reform so late in the presidential election year of 1972, but the bills were a gauntlet thrown down to the members of Congress, intended as a warning signal to all interested parties and to the broad public to gird for battle in 1973.

With the Vietnam war, welfare reform and several other major long-contested subjects fading into the background, tax reform could be a principal issue in the 93rd Congress. The deep ideological conflicts and huge economic interests underlying the issue may turn the debate into a divisive and bitterly fought controversy. Whether the drive for federal income tax reform, which became a national force in the mid-1950s and has remained in the forefront of public interest ever since, will bring decisive action in 1973 remains to be seen.

Why tax reform? Taken at face value, the case for federal tax reform by broadening the income tax base is persuasive: the federal income tax now reaches only about half of all personal income as defined in the national income accounts, and even the taxed half is not always subjected to the full impact of the tax rate schedule. Does it make economic sense or promote "equal justice under the law" to levy rates rising from 14 to 70 percent on *half* of all income when just half of this assessment on *all* income—or a flat rate of 10 percent on all personal income, or a 14 percent rate on "adjusted gross income"—would yield about the same amount of revenue to the government? Might it not cause far less distortion, evasion, and complication to levy lower rates on a broader base? Is it wise for the government to continue to dig deep into personal income with a huge sieve that yields only half of what it is supposed to produce? Most of the complexity in the Internal Revenue Code, which over the years has progressed from intricacy to near incomprehensibility, is the result of two factors: (1) the expansion of the code by too many exclusions, exemptions, deductions, and other devices that whittle down "taxable income"; and (2) differential rates imposed on different types or magnitudes of income. While few would expect to see all tax differentials abolished at one blow, the current complication and apparent unfairness of many provisions seem to clamor for radical simplification.

But broadening the base by subjecting much—or most, or all— of the presently nontaxed income to the tax is far more feasible in theory than it turns out to be in the cold light of political reality, when the task is to be tackled in earnest, item by item. Congressional committees—House Ways and Means, Senate Finance, Joint Economic, Joint Internal Revenue Taxation—have conducted tax reform hearings year after year and have gathered tens of thousands of pages of testimony, but these efforts have produced relatively few tangible results. The fact is that the tax code has grown more complicated every time Congress has attempted to improve it—most recently so with the Tax Reform Act of 1969 which is widely, and justifiedly, called the "Lawyers' and Accountants' Full Employment Act of 1969."

The repeal of special provisions that benefit only a small number of taxpayers may produce good and sometimes dramatic publicity but in most cases will yield only small revenue. On the other hand, provisions that account for the big erosions in the tax base tend to affect millions of taxpayers who, when their established privileges seem threatened, rise in wrath—as individuals, as congressional constituencies, as collective economic interests, or through political, state or national organizations—to defend their existing benefits. What some regard as a "loophole" is to others a birthright, an indispensable lifesaver and a means of achieving tax parity with others.

The why of loopholes. Contrary to what is often asserted and widely believed, the remedial provisions in the tax code are seldom there by accident or oversight, let alone as the result of the sinister machinations of special interest lobbyists who either bribed lawmakers or pulled the wool over the eyes of unsuspecting congressmen and the public. The conspiracy theory of tax law is not convincing in view of the legislative history of each of the provisions involved. Virtually all provisions that shield some income from the full impact of the rate schedule—or from any tax—were put there not by inadvertence, or from ignorance, or as a rule for the purpose of giving some favored groups improper advantages or privileges. Most of the tax differentials aim at one or both of these two objectives:

(1) to provide greater equity, horizontal or vertical, among taxpayers and different types and magnitudes of income by taking into

3

account differing circumstances and offering relief for hardships; (2) to provide incentives to taxpayers to engage in or enlarge activities which are held to be desirable as a matter of public policy. This is done by offering rewards to some and imposing penalties on others.

These two objectives often produce conflicting results when translated into tax policy.

There is a great deal of ambiguity about what constitutes an inequity meriting remedial action and what is desirable public policy calling for governmental or private action. Defenders of special viewpoints or interests almost always present their proposals in the manner of a Western movie: there are the good guys and the bad guys, and nobody can be in doubt as to which is which. But the reality of tax controversies is seldom so black and white; it almost always is a question of differing shades of grey, with more or less reasonable and valid arguments put forth by both sides. The merits or drawbacks of any provision or proposal are rarely if ever as simple as its spokesmen or detractors present them to be.

Perhaps in a very few cases clever manipulators were able to slip a remedial tax provision past an unsuspecting Congress. But such unintended benefits have never remained a secret for very long. If Congress does not favorably respond to the demand of some groups to abolish specified "loopholes," it is not because of a lack of understanding or in deference to secret influences but because the merits of the case are in doubt. Invariably there is another side to the question— problems that the proponents of the particular change do not mention, except in a negative light. If there are not two sides to an issue, then it is really not an issue. When there are no reasons—economic, moral, political or ideological—for objecting to a proposed change, then there is no controversy and the change has a good chance of being accepted.

This does not mean, of course, that all tax provisions as they presently stand necessarily express the informed and balanced judgment of the Congress, or that they are all justifiable and fair. Far from it. But it does mean that when all factors are taken into consideration, the issues are seldom clearcut. Congress must keep the interests of all groups in mind, not only of those with the most effective public relations machinery or organized voting power. It cannot take the claims of one side as the revealed truth without giving a fair hearing to the other side. Time and again Congress finds itself in the position of the

4

judge who, after listening to the plaintiff, nodded to him and said, "You are right." After the defendant had told his story, the judge nodded again and said, "You are right." At that point the clerk of the court approached the bench and whispered in the judge's ear: "But Your Honor, they both can't be right." The judge thought a moment and then nodded to the clerk, "You are right, too."

Neutrality or redistribution? If only material interests were involved, tax conflicts might not be so difficult to resolve. However, frequently the problem centers around deep-seated ideologies, fundamental principles of justice in the distribution of income and wealth, or public policies that do not lend themselves easily to compromise. The principle of "neutrality in taxation," advanced as the epitome of fairness in classic economic thought, has long been honored more in the breach than in observance. While many may think it desirable to leave taxpayers in the same relative position *after* taxes as they were *before*, many others regard such policy as sheer heresy. As a practical matter, neutrality is hardly conceivable given today's political climate and level of taxation. When the tax burden equals no more than 10 to 15 percent of the nation's income as it did in the early part of the twentieth century, a policy of complete neutrality is theoretically, and even politically, feasible. But that is hardly the case when total governmental revenues equal about 40 percent of personal income, as they have for some years in the United States and other industrial nations. Government cannot extract 40 percent of total income and leave all persons in the same *relative* position. Some types of activity cannot sustain such a tax burden without being wiped out—any more than low-income earners could carry such a load and maintain customary living standards.

An even harder division to resolve is the ideological conflict over the government's role in the economy. Some believe that the rewards and punishments of the market are, by and large, merited and fair, and that the highest economic growth is produced by giving market forces the widest possible free rein. To ensure the greatest good for the greatest number of people, then, this faction would wish to leave pre-tax relative positions as undisturbed as possible. But even many advocates of such a free market policy now concede that government may need to provide remedies and relief for those who have fallen by the way-side—whether as a result of impartial forces, the activities of more efficacious groups, or an individual's own fault or contributory negli-

5

gence. The view has become prevalent that it is government's primary task to remedy the imperfections of market decisions, to alter through the political process the rewards and punishments of the free play of market forces. Some have come to regard government chiefly as a huge machine for redistributing income from those who have more to those who have less, no matter what reasons might underlie an individual's poor economic condition. Some degree of egalitarianism has become part of public policy as a logical result of and concomitant with the one man-one vote principle.

By and large, redistribution of income through progressive taxation and social expenditures has become so generally accepted in the United States and everywhere else that the principle as a rule of public policy is no longer seriously questioned.[1] But it is not at all decided just how far government should go in taking a larger slice from those who produce and earn, and in giving to those who produce less or nothing. How far can government go, for example, without weakening incentives? Should the tax structure be made more progressive than it is, or less? Many, and possibly most, persons and organizations judge a broad-scaled tax proposal by one criterion: does it tend to redistribute more income, or do so more effectively, from those who have more to those who have less? Most arguments over tax issues are shaped, most battle lines are drawn, and most decisions are arrived at by that criterion. All other issues, though they may consume much time and space in the debate, shrink in true significance before the one overriding issue: does the proposal take more from the rich and does it give more to the poor?

The Movement for Income Tax Reform

Though it adopted an income tax much later than most industrial countries, the United States has come to lean on this particular tax as the major source of public revenue far more heavily than other nations. Broad-scaled general consumption taxation, which forms the backbone of government budgets in Europe and most everywhere else, has never gained acceptance in the United States, at least not as a federal tax, though it has been and probably will remain a subject of periodic dis-

---

[1] But the principle as such is at times questioned. Walter J. Blum and Harry Kalven, Jr., *The Uneasy Case for Progressive Taxation* (Chicago: University of Chicago Press, 1953).

cussion. Short of a fiscal emergency, imposition of a major national consumption tax does not now appear very likely in the immediate future. Hence the income tax is economically, socially and politically more important in America than elsewhere—and, incidentally, also more complicated and controversial, if not in principle then in application and structure.

First imposed in 1913 at rates from 1 to 7 percent, principally on only a small number of wealthy persons, the income tax was turned from a class tax into a mass tax during World War I when the levy was extended downward to reach low incomes and its rate scale elevated to between 6 and 77 percent. The 1920s saw a series of reductions in the rate scale to a low of between 0.5 and 24 percent by 1929, a downward trend that was reversed in the 1930s and during World War II when the scale climbed to its highest level ever—from 23 to 94 percent—and the number of taxpayers multiplied tenfold. Tax cuts in the immediate postwar period were quite small and it was not until 1964 that the 14 to 70 percent scale was adopted which is still in effect. Meanwhile, the Internal Revenue Code and regulations grew in size with the addition of a myriad of provisions of unparalleled complexity.

In the years following World War II much attention was directed toward the use of taxes, particularly the income tax, as an instrument of countercyclical fiscal policy. Concern focused on the macroeconomic use of taxation so that tax policy would offer the least obstacle to, and as far as possible would serve to stimulate, steady economic expansion. The Council of Economic Advisers, the Joint Economic Committee of Congress and the President's annual economic report—all created by the Employment Act of 1946—guided the debate toward a goal of maximum employment of the country's manpower and other resources, as well as stimulation of other areas of national growth in which tax policy was to play a significant role. Shortly after the recodification of the Internal Revenue Code in 1954, the Joint Economic Committee conducted what was up to that time probably the country's most comprehensive and intensive tax study: *Federal Tax Policy for Economic Growth and Stability* (1955). Very few of the experts who prepared papers and participated in the panel discussions referred to what became the prime subject of the tax debate in later years—namely, "erosion of the tax base and rate structure." Only limited attention was paid to the subject at the time.

7

Erosion of the tax base. Interest in this problem increased and gradually, in the second half of the 1950s, turned into a drive for income tax reform by broadening the tax base. At the 1955 annual conference of the National Tax Association, Joseph A. Pechman presented a paper subsequently expanded into an article and published in 1957 under the title, "Erosion of the Individual Income Tax."[2] Mr. Pechman demonstrated that only about 40 percent of *personal* income appeared on federal income tax returns as *taxable* income and estimated that out of personal income of $325 billion in 1956, $189 billion was untaxed:

	Billions
Social insurance and public welfare, wages "in kind," imputed rental on owner-occupied homes, interest on state and local bonds, et cetera	$ 35
Personal exemptions on taxable returns ($600 per head)	77
Excess of personal exemptions and deductions over income on nontaxable returns and "no returns" . .	17
Standard deductions	13
Itemized deductions (mostly state and local taxes, charitable contributions, interest and medical expenses)	21
Unreported income	26
	$189

It is immediately apparent that the bulk of the $198 billion of nontaxed 1956 income was received by persons in the lower income brackets and that only a small percentage of the total redounded to the benefit of wealthy persons. That clearly was and remains the intent of the law.

Mr. Pechman suggested that at least part of the nontaxed income, in all groups, be included in a more comprehensive tax base which would make it possible to reduce tax rates across the board. His appeal caught on rapidly. Within a few years, the concepts of the eroded tax base and untaxed income attained wide public attention, were prominently featured in the media, and finally were placed on the agenda of Congress. As the debate reached the political level, attention shifted sharply from the hundreds of billions of untaxed income—one-half or

---

[2] See *National Tax Journal,* March 1957. Mr. Pechman, who was then with the Council of Economic Advisers, later joined the Committee for Economic Development and now is with the Brookings Institution.

more of all personal income—to provisions whose impact is far smaller in magnitude but which directly benefit mostly persons in the higher income brackets. This is where the focus of the tax reform movement has remained ever since. It has become not so much a drive to broaden the tax base as to tax the wealthy more heavily.

The House Ways and Means Committee's 1958 hearings on *General Revenue Revision,* extensive as they were (3,600 pages), are part of the "pre-reform" era: they dealt mostly with undue tax impact on certain industries. Soon afterwards though, the committee's new chairman, Representative Wilbur Mills, cleared the decks for a major attack on loopholes, as the drive for tax reform soon came to be known. His oft-quoted article—"Are You a Pet or a Patsy? Our Unfair Tax Laws Coddle Some But Force Others to Pay Through the Nose" [3]—set the pattern for a vigorous study of and campaign for income tax reform. Ways and Means Committee hearings in 1959, to which nearly 200 witnesses were invited (including some of the most prominent American tax experts), aimed at a broadening of the tax base and repeal of special preferences and deductions. They covered virtually every type of income not subject to the full impact of the rate schedule, every type of exclusion, exemption, deduction, credit or preference, and brought forth an infinite variety of ideas and proposals on desired improvements in the income tax. The resulting *Tax Revision Compendium* composed of papers submitted, panel discussions and summaries, still is, more than a dozen years later, the most comprehensive discussion of the major aspects of American income taxation. But contrary to the hopes and expectations of its sponsors this most ambitious effort at tax reform resulted in no legislative action whatsoever in the succeeding four years. It was a splendid academic exercise—and so it remained.

When one of the most knowledgeable and articulate advocates of "loophole closing," Professor Stanley S. Surrey of the Harvard Law School, was appointed assistant secretary of the Treasury for tax policy in 1961, it might have been expected that major proposals for comprehensive tax reform would soon be forthcoming. But although Mr. Surrey devoted much of his considerable energy to the task in the succeeding eight years, very few of his ideas were put into practice. President Kennedy's two tax messages—April 20, 1961, and January 24, 1963—mentioned structural reform and referred to such items as

---

[3] *Life,* November 23, 1959.

tightened capital gains taxation, a floor under itemized deductions and an end to unlimited charitable deductions. But these were minor subjects in messages whose main emphasis was on incentives to stimulate economic growth by tax concessions. "The chief problem confronting our economy in 1963 is its unrealized potential—slow growth, under-investment, unused capacity and persistent unemployment." [4] By far the most important tax proposal adopted was a business investment credit—which some observers have been calling another big loophole ever since its introduction in 1962. In contrast to widespread criticism of the eroding tax base during and subsequent to the 1959 hearings, President Kennedy declared in 1961: "This message recognizes the basic soundness of our tax structure." [5] It is not surprising that only very few minor suggestions among the limited number of structural recommendations survived.

The bill passed by Congress in 1964 was mainly a tax reduction act that freed an additional 1.5 million persons of any tax liability, cut taxes for most other taxpayers (particularly in the lower brackets), and widened rather than narrowed the range and amount of income exempt from taxation. Nor is that surprising: to most taxpayers tax reform means tax relief. This is why the experience of 1964 was repeated in 1969 and in 1971: what had been announced as an attempt at tax reform became basically action to reduce taxes for the great mass of voters in the middle and lower income brackets and to end any liability for millions in the lowest income categories. The tax reform drive promised to offset revenue losses at the bottom of the income scale by substantial tax boosts in the high brackets through repeal, or at least a sharp reduction, of provisions benefiting well-to-do taxpayers. Considering the broad popular appeal and publicity value of such an approach and, above all, the relative size and voting strength of the two constituencies, this seemed to be a well-designed strategy. Resistance to change from the small number of taxpayers at the upper end was to be overcome by approval from larger numbers in the lower brackets.

Estimates of potential revenue gains from tax reform were commonly based on the assumption that the tax changes would not affect the nature and volume of transactions and that, for example, sale of assets, oil exploration programs and bond markets would go on as they had before. Opponents questioned the assumption that operations would

---

[4] *Congressional Record,* January 24, 1963, p. 962.
[5] *Congressional Record,* April 20, 1961, p. 6456.

continue undisturbed and that the promised revenue gains would in fact materialize.

Federal revenue needs soared in the second half of the 1960s, as expenditures jumped from $118 billion in 1965 to $197 billion in 1970 and a huge budgetary deficit loomed ahead (it actuallly totaled $25 billion in fiscal year 1968). To meet this problem, President Johnson, in a message to Congress of August 3, 1967, proposed a $7.4 billion tax boost—not by closing some of the much-discussed loopholes but principally by a temporary across-the-board 10 percent surcharge on the existing tax liabilities of individuals and corporations. Treasury officials had repeatedly emphasized the unused revenue potential of tax reform. Yet now they chose to seek the needed funds by other means. The probable explanation for this reversal is that when the chips were down and the money was badly needed, officials did not rate revenue potential from reform as high—in a realistic evaluation—as they had in some of the other pronouncements on the need for broadening the tax base and tax reform. Congress seemed to agree, too: it imposed a 10 percent surtax but did not touch tax reform.

Though there was no presidential or congressional action on tax reform for about five years following the passage of the Revenue Act of 1964, intensive work continued in the Treasury under the direction of Assistant Secretary for Tax Policy Stanley S. Surrey. Under a congressional mandate to the President to submit tax reform proposals before the end of 1968, a major staff report with recommendations was prepared. But President Johnson decided not to transmit the proposals to Congress and they were made public only at the request of Congress sometime later, after the new administration had taken office. But, like its predecessor, the Nixon administration did not make the Treasury staff proposals on loophole-closing its own.

The Barr bomb. Two days before leaving office, Secretary of the Treasury Joseph Barr—who served in that capacity for the 31-day interim between Henry Fowler's resignation and David M. Kennedy's assumption of office—delivered a blow that reverberated for a long time and made the tax reform drive a major political force in 1969. On January 17, Secretary Barr issued a stern warning to the Joint Economic Committee of Congress: the country was facing a taxpayers' revolt, not because taxes were so high, but because rich people were not paying their fair share; 155 taxpayers with an adjusted gross income of

11

$200,000 or more had paid no income tax in 1967, among them 21 persons with an income of $1 million or more. Mr. Barr's statement—delivered without an explanation of why or how recipients of huge gross incomes could escape paying taxes—was prominently featured in news media throughout the country and aroused public sentiment to a high pitch. The result was a situation not too different from the tax-payers' revolt that he had predicted. Some members of Congress who had viewed tax reform with detachment early in the session came back from Easter recess with a mandate from their constituents and a personal determination to "make the rich pay."

On February 18, 1969, about a month before President Nixon submitted 16 minor tax reform proposals (with an insignificant revenue effect) to the Congress, the House Ways and Means Committee began tax reform hearings on such subjects as tax-exempt charitable foundations, capital gains, interest on state and local bonds, and depletion allowances. With the new impetus, the committee extended its purview and the House passed a huge tax bill on August 8. The Senate acted even faster and the President signed the measure on December 30, 1969. The 225-page bill, the biggest and most complex addition to the Internal Revenue Code ever, made hundreds of changes in the tax law.

Tax reform in 1969 and 1971. The Tax Reform Act of 1969 was the first genuine attempt to come to grips with the type of tax reform that had been advocated for about 15 years. But in terms of the announced goals of the loophole-closing drive, it was at best a very cautious first step that did not go very far and avoided the "tough" issues. Among other things, the act reduced the gas and oil depletion allowance from 27.5 to 22 percent, tightened the availability of the 25 percent capital gains tax, established a minimum tax on income with limited tax preferences (LTP) and imposed a 4-percent tax on the net investment income of tax-exempt foundations. But all of this was dwarfed by the tax reductions the act granted: an increase in the personal exemption to $750, an increase in the standard deduction to 15 percent with a maximum of $2,000 (from 10 percent and $1,000), a reduction from 70 to 50 percent in the top rate on *earned* income and a maximum tax for single persons that cannot exceed 120 percent of what they would pay if they were married. In the aggregate, the tax liability of returns in the lowest income bracket was cut by 70 percent (i.e., to less than one-third), that

12

of returns in the highest bracket raised by 7 percent. More than 9 million persons were dropped from the tax rolls altogether.

Though it was announced as an attempt to broaden the tax base, the Tax Reform Act of 1969 increased the percentage of personal income that is *not* reached by the federal income tax by 2 percentage points—from 48.2 percent in 1969 to 50.2 in 1970. Two years later, in December 1971, another revenue bill was enacted that consisted almost exclusively of tax cuts. It not only accelerated some of the relief provided for in the 1969 act but also added numerous other remedial provisions. The 1971 measure permitted credit for political contributions for the first time, greatly liberalized child care deductions, introduced a job development investment credit and reintroduced the 7 percent investment credit. Revenue losses from the 1969 and 1971 acts have contributed substantially to recent budgetary deficits. The unified budget deficit ran between $23 and $25 billion in the fiscal years 1971 and 1972, and may be this high again in 1973. Deficits give all signs of becoming a permanent feature of our fiscal system.

Tax "expenditures"? Spokesmen for the tax reform drive meanwhile continued to point out that huge amounts were being lost each year to the Treasury through tax concessions. Assistant Treasury Secretary Stanley S. Surrey developed the concept of *tax expenditures*—government expenditures made through the tax system—and continued to promote this concept after he left office in January 1969. Most of the tax deductions, exclusions, exemptions, and credits, Surrey theorized, are the equivalent of public expenditures for the benefited purposes, and they ought to be treated as such and subjected to the same type of annual review by the Congress and the executive branch as other expenditures. Ways and Means Committee Chairman Wilbur Mills referred to such tax concessions as "a form of backdoor spending." Surrey subsequently prepared an estimated "Tax Expenditure Budget" which placed the total between $42 and $45 billion for fiscal year 1968.[6] In 1972 he estimated that the federal government would spend from $55 to $60 billion a year through tax breaks.[7]

More recently, tax concessions have been called *tax subsidies* and

---

[6] *Annual Report of the Secretary of the Treasury on the State of the Finances,* for the Fiscal Year ended June 30, 1968 (Washington, D.C.: U.S. Government Printing Office, 1969), pp. 326-40.

[7] *Wall Street Journal,* April 12, 1972.

have been included in studies of federal subsidy programs. The staff of the Joint Economic Committee of Congress estimated the gross budgetary cost of major federal tax subsidies in fiscal year 1971 at $35.8 billion.[8] At the committee's hearings held in January 1972, Joseph A. Pechman and Benjamin A. Okner of the Brookings Institution estimated that a comprehensive income tax would yield $180 billion in 1972—about $77 billion more than the estimated $103 billion yield under current law.[9] Such a 75 percent increase in the aggregate income tax receipts would more than triple the tax liability of persons in the lowest brackets (under $5,000) and nearly double the tax of those in the top brackets ($500,000 and up).

Assistant Secretary of the Treasury for Economic Policy Murray Weidenbaum testified on June 2, 1970, before the Joint Economic Committee's Subcommittee on Economy in Government, that tax aids—a term he preferred to tax expenditures—totaled more than $44 billion in fiscal year 1969. This estimate was brought up to date by Under Secretary of the Treasury Edwin S. Cohen appearing before the Joint Economic Committee on July 21, 1972. Cohen warned that many of the estimates were merely tentative, that each provision was computed independently of any other, that therefore an addition of the separate estimates might not produce meaningful figures and that no consideration was given to the likely impact of such tax changes on investment patterns and activity. With these caveats, he put the total for special tax provisions in calendar year 1971 at $51.7 billion in revenue, of which $41.8 billion came under individual income tax and $9.9 billion under corporate profits tax. Major individual income tax items in Cohen's estimate included:

	Billions
Untaxed part of capital gains	$5.6
Deductions for:	
Home mortgages and property taxes	5.1
Other state and local nonbusiness taxes	5.6
Charitable contributions	3.2

[8] U.S. Congress, Joint Economic Committee, *The Economics of Federal Subsidy Programs,* a staff study (Washington, D.C.: U. S. Government Printing Office, January 1972), p. 31.
[9] U.S. Congress, Joint Economic Committee, *The Economics of Federal Subsidy Programs,* Hearings before the Subcommittee on Priorities and Economy in Government (Washington, D.C.: U.S. Government Printing Office, January 1972), p. 71.

	Billions
Interest on consumer debt	1.8
Excluded pension contributions	3.7
Interest on municipal bonds	.8
Excess of percentage over cost depletion	.2
Exclusion of social security, unemployment compensation, welfare, et cetera	4.7

Estimates of the cost of special provisions—whether they be called tax expenditures, tax subsidies, tax aids, loopholes, or whatever—vary widely because they are based on value judgments rooted in political philosophy. Each author has a different concept of what items should be included in the list and how much revenue could be derived from their repeal; each excludes some major items of nontaxed income accruing to persons in the middle and lower brackets. All agree, however, that the Treasury's loss from these provisions is huge. At a time when large annual budget deficits pose grave inflationary risks, thought might be given to narrowing future deficits by closing or tightening some of the "tax loopholes."

More revenue from tax reform? Recent projections of the federal budget outlook paint a gloomy picture. A group of Brookings Institution economists led by Charles L. Schultze predicted, on the basis of the President's budget for fiscal year 1973, continued huge deficits through 1975 and a possible balanced budget (assuming full employment conditions) by 1977.[10] When Congress subsequently passed a 20 percent social security increase (instead of the 5 percent recommended by the President) and voted other spending increases, the Brookings authors revised their estimates upwards. An article by Alice M. Rivlin, "Dear Voter: Your taxes are going up (no matter who wins on Tuesday)," and a speech by Charles Schultze predicted large deficits through 1976 with a possible excess of revenue in the years after fiscal 1978.[11] This latter forecast was based on the assumption that receipts would grow faster than expenditures, an assumption that receives little encouragement from the record of recent years. The authors cited the massive pressures for new and expanded programs—forces that might prevail and, if they did so, would make illusory any prediction about receipts

---

[10] Charles L. Schultze et al., *Setting National Priorities: The 1973 Budget* (Washington, D.C.: The Brookings Institution, 1972).

[11] See, respectively, *New York Times Magazine,* November 5, 1972, and *Congressional Record,* October 16, 1972, pp. E 8743–8747.

growing more rapidly than expenditures. About the same time, the American Enterprise Institute's long-range budget project, comprised of David J. Ott and several associates, predicted similar results: unless taxes are boosted, large-scale deficits are to be expected until 1977 (even under full employment conditions) and thus at best a modest surplus cannot materialize until 1978 or after.[12]

Could those expected deficits be met through tax reform? Joseph A. Pechman and Benjamin A. Okner discussed the possibility of having Congress close several loopholes and came up with a modest additional annual yield ranging from $3.1 to $10.2 billion.[13] In other words, even strong proponents of tax reform are not optimistic about the actual revenue potential involved.

To be sure, the subject of tax reform came up repeatedly in the 1972 congressional session and during the presidential campaign. One of the major proposals for reform (S. 3378)—introduced in March 1972 by 12 senators including Senators McGovern, Humphrey, Muskie, Kennedy and Nelson—was designed "to raise needed revenue" estimated at $16 billion. The bill called for 55 changes, such as taxing unrealized capital gains at death (with later provisions to tax as ordinary income), reducing percentage depletion on oil from 22 to 15 percent, inducing state and local governments to issue taxable bonds, repealing accelerated real estate depreciation, and repealing $100 dividend exclusion. In the House, H.R. 13877, sponsored by 59 members, aimed to raise an additional $7.25 billion by similar but less far-reaching changes. The most drastic proposals were the Mills-Mansfield bills mentioned above (H.R. 15230 and S. 3657 introduced in May 1972) which called for the repeal of 54 major tax provisions in installments of 18 each in January 1974, 1975 and 1976.

It came as no surprise when tax reform was injected into the presidential campaign in the form of an appeal to tax high income people more severely. In a New York speech on August 29, Senator McGovern announced that as President he "would seek a fair-share tax reform to raise approximately $22 billion in additional revenues by 1975," mostly from the high tax brackets while persons with middle or

---

[12] David J. Ott et al., *Nixon, McGovern and the Federal Budget* (Washington, D.C.: American Enterprise Institute, 1972).
[13] "Alternative Sources of Federal Revenue," in Schultze et al., *Setting National Priorities*, p. 433.

lower incomes would pay less.[14] A subsequent statement spelled out his proposals in further detail, proposals that paralleled in many respects those contained in the above-mentioned bills. As it turned out, however, tax reform played no significant role in the 1972 presidential campaign. President Nixon had said in his September 1971 request for tax legislation that he would send tax reform proposals to Congress in 1972. But in February 1972, Secretary of the Treasury John Connally had suggested that a presidential campaign year was not a good time to consider tax reform, an issue that should be studied in a cooler and less passionate atmosphere. The President indicated subsequently that his tax reform goals would be spelled out in a special message early in 1973.

Current prospects are that presidential proposals will be forthcoming in the spring of 1973 and will be subjected to extensive congressional hearings. These proposals are not likely to go as far as some of the suggestions made by Democratic party spokesmen in 1972—or by leading advocates of tax reform—and may not involve major revenue gains. If large additional revenues are needed for budgetary purposes in 1973 and in subsequent years, as it now appears, Congress will most likely vote a broad increase in income taxes, such as a surtax, rather than repeal so-called tax loopholes.

The fiscal battle will probably be fought out over income taxes because they dominate the federal tax picture. In recent years, individual and corporate income taxes have produced between 60 and 65 percent of *all* revenues in the unified budget. But this budget includes revenues earmarked for social insurance, highway and other trust funds and therefore not available for general fiscal purposes. If trust fund revenues are excluded (as they were in the administrative budget which was replaced by the unified budget in 1969), income taxes supply about 85 percent of federal revenues. According to Census Bureau definitions and statistics, income taxes have accounted for 80 to 85 percent of all federal tax revenues for the past two decades—with two-thirds to three-quarters of the receipts coming from the individual income tax, the remainder from the corporate profits tax. This shows a far heavier reliance on in-

---

[14] "From McGovern: A New Blueprint for Taxes, Welfare," *U. S. News & World Report,* September 11, 1972; "McGovern's Tax Plan: 22 Billions More by 1975," *U. S. News & World Report,* October 2, 1972; John F. Burby, "Complex McGovern Economics Plan Dissolves in Campaign Heat," *National Journal,* September 16, 1972.

come taxation than in other countries. In fact, the United States is the only industrial nation that does not levy a broad-based consumption tax as a major source of national revenue. It is because of this lopsidedness in our federal tax system that the imposition of a consumption tax, such as a value-added tax, has repeatedly been proposed. But there is a major objection to such a tax: in contrast to the individual income tax, it does *not* redistribute income from the rich to the poor and may well be regressive with respect to income. This argument is a powerful political factor that raises considerable doubt as to whether a national consumption tax can soon be adopted in the United States except in a dire fiscal emergency or in an atmosphere different from that prevailing today.

This leaves four other possible solutions to the budgetary problem in the next few years. Congress could control expenditure growth more effectively than it has shown an inclination to do. But, according to some recent studies, this is not very likely to happen. Congress could, on the other hand, let the large annual deficits that have prevailed in fiscal years 1971, 1972 and 1973 continue into the future, permitting them to become a fixture of the federal fiscal system through the 1970s. To restrain the resulting inflationary pressures, it might then be found necessary to tighten, and extend indefinitely, wage-price and other economic controls instead of gradually relaxing and finally repealing them. A third possibility would be to boost income taxes by raising rates or imposing a surtax to produce the needed revenue, as was done in 1968. Fourth, and least likely, Congress could subject some of the major now-protected forms of personal income to the full impact of the tax rate schedule in a move toward developing a comprehensive tax base (CTB).

Theoretically, tax reform could be enacted on its own, so as to produce additional revenue, rather than be coupled with a tax cut. However, a review of the record of recent decades casts considerable doubt on the revenue potential of tax reform. No matter how tax reform has started out, it has always wound up as tax reduction. But, then, history never quite repeats itself. While the emphasis and force of the tax reform drive are likely to remain on the elusive and controversial concept of equity, there is at least a possibility, slim as it may be, that reform could also help to narrow the huge budgetary deficits that have characterized the past few years. This obviously would call for courageous and disciplined action on the part of Congress.

18

Do the Rich Pay No Income Taxes?

The tax reform movement gained its greatest strength in 1969 when the issue moved to the front pages of the metropolitan dailies and held the center stage of national attention. Public demand for congressional action reached a crescendo as never before, or after. By the end of the year, feverish action of the tax-writing committees and of both houses of Congress had produced the most extensive and far-reaching tax changes ever. But in terms of its declared objectives, the tax reform drive achieved so little in the Tax Reform Act of 1969 that it may be said that "the mountains labored and brought forth a tiny mouse."

A tempest over taxes. As has been noted, the single event that sparked the tax reform drive in 1969, a veritable bombshell, was Joseph Barr's statement before the Joint Economic Committee just two days before relinquishing the office of secretary of the Treasury. Barr said:

> We face now the possibility of a taxpayer revolt if we do not soon make major reforms in our income taxes. The revolt will come not from the poor but from the tens of millions of middle-class families and individuals with incomes of $7,000 to $20,000, whose tax payments now generally are based on the full ordinary rates and who pay over half of our individual income taxes.

> The middle classes are likely to revolt against income taxes not because of the level or amount of the taxes they must pay but because certain provisions of the tax laws unfairly lighten the burdens of others who can afford to pay. People are concerned and indeed angered about the high-income recipients who pay little or no Federal income taxes. For example, the extreme cases are 155 tax returns in 1967 with adjusted gross incomes above $200,000 on which no Federal income taxes were paid, including 21 with incomes above $1,000,000.[15]

Barr's charges were played up by the media and kept the pot boiling for many months:

> As an unprecedented amount of mail seconding Barr poured into the Treasury and Congress, it finally seemed the long-lost cause of tax reform was an idea whose time had come. House Ways and Means Committee Chairman Wilbur

---

[15] Statement of Joseph W. Barr, January 17, 1969, in *The 1969 Economic Report of the President,* Hearings before the Joint Economic Committee (Washington, D.C.: U.S. Government Printing Office, 1969), p. 46.

Mills scheduled exhaustive hearings to prepare legislative proposals, and the new Nixon administration seemed ready to
make tax reform one of its domestic priorities. (*Life*, April 4,
1969)

The plain fact was that middle-income Americans, faced
with the biggest peacetime tax bite in memory, were expres-
sing their discontent in an ever-swelling volume of angry mail
inundating Capitol Hill. What particularly galled the taxpayers
was a system that was hitting them harder than ever while
permitting a wealthy few to escape with relatively little tax or
even none at all. (*Newsweek*, February 17, 1969)

Mr. Nixon, in the weeks before he sent his tax-reform
message to Congress, was receiving reports from all around
the country that public anger about taxes had become the
hottest political topic in the U.S., topping such things as
Vietnam, crime, and the cost of living (*U.S. News & World
Report*, May 5, 1969)

In sum, today's taxes tend to broaden the gulf between
rich and poor, landlord and tenant, worker and entrepreneur.
What upsets Americans most is the feeling they are being
cheated. . . . (*Time*, April 4, 1969)

. . . the House Ways and Means Committee will begin
hearings on a long list of proposals not only to shut off the
escape routes used by the rich and crafty but to make the
rules apply more equitably to all. . . .
But the biggest inequity remains the perfectly legal way
the rich and super-rich shortage the IRS with financial razzle-
dazzle. . . . The rich can wipe out a large part or even all of
their tax liability by using one of several forms of personal
deductions allowed by the code. (*Newsweek*, February 24,
1969)

It is understandable that such a sensational story—the very rich
escape income taxes—emanating from the secretary of the Treasury (if
only in office for 31 days) would create a national sensation. For whatever reason, Barr did not disclose the methods or specific code provisions that enabled those high-income earners to avoid any tax liability,
although he must have known what they were or could easily have found
out. By adding mystery, further attention was drawn to the alleged
injustices of the tax system and the matter was left open for wild
speculation and for pointed accusations not only against the individuals
involved, but against all rich people as tax evaders—and, of course,

Table 1
SHARES OF THE FEDERAL INDIVIDUAL INCOME TAX
By MAJOR INCOME BRACKETS, 1970

Adjusted Gross Income Bracket	Share of Adjusted Gross Income	Share of Tax Liability
Under $7,000	19.5%	10.5%
$7,000 to $19,999	59.2	54.0
$20,000 and over	21.3	35.5
	100.0%	100.0%

Source: Internal Revenue Service, *Statistics of Income, 1970, Individual Income Tax Returns* (Preliminary), 1972; hereafter cited as IRS, *Statistics of Income, 1970.*

against Congress for permitting such a scandal. The fact that the charges were sweeping and the underlying facts obscured enhanced the inflammatory nature of the attack. It was not until a few years later that the Treasury disclosed the results of investigations into high-bracket income tax returns with no tax liability. Treasury Under Secretary Edwin S. Cohen made the facts public in 1972.[16] Some of the factual background is also available from statistical data regularly published by the Internal Revenue Service.

There is no evidence that the middle classes actually bear a disproportionate share of the federal income tax as Barr asserted. In 1970, for instance, they received 59 percent of adjusted gross income and paid 54 percent of the tax (see Table 1). There also may be some doubt about the allegation that the ire of the middle classes (or of the taxpayers in general) is not directed at "the level or amount of taxes they must pay," particularly at a time when the aggregate total of all taxes and governmental revenues equals 41 percent of all personal income in the United States.[17]

---

[16] *Congressional Record,* February 9, 1972, p. H 963; Mr. Cohen's speech on April 29, 1972 (Boston), as well as his testimony before the Joint Economic Committee, July 21, 1972 (with appendixes) and his speech on September 26, 1972 (New York).

[17] Governmental expenditures equaled about 44 percent of personal income in 1971 which suggests that the taxpayer may not have seen the worst yet, if at some time in the future governmental income should be raised to balance outgo. No information has been available on size distribution of personal income since 1964. Therefore, adjusted gross income (AGI) is used as the only available base.

21

Do the rich go free? For 1970, a total of 15,323 individual income tax returns were filed with an adjusted gross income (AGI) of $200,000 or more; 15,211 of those returns or 99.3 percent were taxable. Combined adjusted gross income on these taxable returns totalled $6.2 billion, taxable income (TI) $4.5 billion, and income tax $2.7 billion. Each taxpayer paid, on the average, a tax of $177,161, equal to 44 percent of his adjusted gross income and 60 percent of his taxable income.

There were 112 returns in the $200,000-and-over adjusted gross income class, with a combined adjusted gross income totalling $47.5 million, that reported *no* tax liability. Since all of the income on these returns was offset by various types of mitigative provisions, the tax-payers in question reported no *taxable* income and therefore paid no tax.

Among the high-bracket returns there were 624 that reported adjusted gross income of $1 million or more. Of these, 621 or 99.5 percent were taxable. Each individual involved paid, on the average, $984,862 in income tax, equal to 46 percent of his adjusted gross income and 65 percent of his taxable income. The aggregate adjusted gross income for this group totalled $1.3 billion, the taxable income $936 million, and the income tax $612 million. This leaves three returns with adjusted gross income of $1 million or more, with a combined adjusted gross income of $10.2 million, that reported no tax liability.

The above figures, of course, are based on pre-audit data. Pre-liminary reports indicate that many of the returns that were nontaxable as submitted will eventually, as the result of audit review, have to pay some, or even sizeable, income taxes.

In summary, well over 99 percent of all high-income bracket returns for 1970 paid high income taxes. Between 0.5 and 0.7 percent of all returns reported that they had no tax liability—a figure that is likely to be whittled down somewhat by subsequent audits. Out of total adjusted gross income of $6.2 billion in the high bracket ($200,000 adjusted gross income and over), $47 million or 0.8 percent was on returns reported to be nontaxable. That leaves one question: why could 112 tax returns with an adjusted gross income of $200,000 and over—and three returns with an adjusted gross income of $1 million or over—claim no income tax liability. Before going into specifics, a few words must be said about definitions and reporting procedures.

According to the Internal Revenue Code, an individual must include in his reported adjusted gross income "all income from whatever source derived," with specified exceptions. It is the procedures for arriving at adjusted gross income that create some of the confusion about loopholes. In the case of profits from a business or profession, the taxpayer lists his gross receipts on Schedule C and deducts his cost of doing business. He includes his resulting *net* income (or loss) in his adjusted gross income. For example, if he has gross receipts of $100,000 and expenses of $80,000, he includes only $20,000 in his adjusted gross income. But in a different case, for example, that of an investor who is not engaged in a regular business operation, Schedule C is not used and the taxpayer must include all of his *gross* receipts in his adjusted gross income. Suppose that John Brown earns a return of $1 million on $10 million he borrowed and invested; he then reports $1 million adjusted gross income. But if the $10 million he borrowed cost him $800,000 in interest, the *net* income on which he can be taxed is only $200,000. Under existing procedures he deducts the $800,000 interest not *before* reporting his adjusted gross income at $1 million but *afterwards*, as an itemized deduction.[18] He only *appears* to be a millionaire, due to a technicality in the law, but actually he is merely a conduit. If he has other offsets against his $200,000 net profit on this transaction—such as capital losses, loss carryovers, casualty losses, bad debts—or if any number of other factors are involved (for example, transactions in a foreign country that are taxed by that country), he may *under unusual circumstances* wind up with no net tax liability.

Since we are considering here returns that account for only a fraction of one percent of all returns, we are truly dealing with exceptional cases. Moreover, the fact that some returns report adjusted gross income of $1 million or more but owe no income tax does not necessarily indicate deviousness or inequity. To repeat, if interest payable on amounts borrowed for more profitable investment and similar items were deductible *before* computing adjusted gross income rather than *after,* many or most of the high adjusted gross income returns in question would no longer be in the no-tax category. The fact is that, in 1970, interest paid was the principal deduction that accounted for nontaxability on 55 nontaxable high adjusted gross income returns (half the total returns of this type). A minor procedural change would eliminate many returns from the high adjusted gross income nontaxable

---

[18] If, however, the interest he paid *exceeds* his investment income by more than $25,000, it may be disallowed as a deduction, from 1972 on.

statistics without in any way altering the substantive provisions of the income tax.

There are a number of other major reasons why 112 high adjusted gross income returns reported no taxable income for 1970. In seven cases nontaxability was due primarily to foreign tax credits. This means that the income arose from transactions in a foreign country and was taxed there, and that, by statute and sometimes under mutual treaties against double taxation, credit for those tax payments was given in the United States. If such income were taxed by both countries, American citizens would find it virtually impossible to engage in business activities abroad. No business can survive if it is taxed twice at rates up to 70 percent.

Twelve high-bracket individuals paid no federal income tax because their deductions for state and local taxes—mostly state income taxes— exceeded their adjusted gross income. Most of the 12 had had large amounts of nonrecurring income in 1969 on which high state income taxes were payable in 1970 and deductible on 1970 federal income tax returns. Treasury investigation found that, in 11 of the 12 cases, the individuals had paid an average of $1.6 million each in federal income taxes in 1969. The coincidence of high income in 1969 and low income in 1970 produced unusual results of this type in less than one return per 1,000 high adjusted gross income returns.

In another dozen cases, large charitable deductions were the principal reason behind nontaxability for 1970. To be sure, the former "unlimited" charitable deductions (for taxpayers who had paid out at least 90 percent of their income in contributions and income taxes in eight of the preceding ten years) were phased out by the Tax Reform Act of 1969 and replaced by a limitation up to 50 percent of adjusted gross income. But there are a few cases where charitable contributions —when added to deductions such as interest, taxes, medical expenses and casualty losses—equal or exceed adjusted gross income. Those returns are therefore nontaxable.

In 20 cases nontaxability was due to "miscellaneous deductions" (the last item on Schedule A), for example, loss of securities pledged to secure loans, losses on guarantee of loans, payments in settlement of litigation, accounting costs, management, counseling and professional fees, and so forth. These are the kinds of items that an operating business would report on Schedule C and therefore could deduct *prior* to computing adjusted gross income. But individual investors have no way of offsetting such costs against earnings except by the use of item-ized deductions *after* adjusted gross income. This could be, and possibly should be, changed by amending the rules. In the meantime, some of those cases will continue to appear in the statistics as high income earners who pay no income tax.

There is other compelling evidence that the 112 tax returns in question are the result of unusual circumstances in a particular year and not of clever manipulations by rich people who regularly manage to escape income taxes: only 12 of the 112 individuals with nontaxable returns for 1970 were also in the nontaxable category in 1966 (when tax returns were studied during consideration of the 1969 Tax Reform Act). In other words, less than one high adjusted gross income tax return in a thousand was nontaxable in both 1966 and 1970.

If we look at all nontaxable returns, not just high income bracket re-turns, we get a far more comprehensive picture (see Table 2). For 1970, about one tax return in every five was nontaxable. Ninety-seven percent of all these nontaxable returns reported an adjusted gross income of less than $5,000. In fact, over one-half of all income tax returns with an adjusted gross income under $5,000 were nontaxable. Only 1 percent of all tax returns with adjusted gross income of $5,000 or more showed no tax liability. The high incidence of nontaxability in the under $5,000 adjusted gross income bracket is of course no accident. It reflects the intent of Congress to tax low-income persons lightly or not at all. But, by all appearances, it is no less the intent of Congress that, in certain unusual circumstances or combinations of circumstances, *some* returns with an adjusted gross income of $10,000 and over be

Table 2
TAXABLE AND NONTAXABLE INCOME TAX RETURNS, 1970

Adjusted Gross Income Class	Number of All Returns	Number of Nontaxable Returns	Percent of Returns Nontaxable	Percent of All Returns
Total	74,285,982	14,949,114	20.1%	100.0%
Under $5,000	28,302,078	14,482,948	51.2	96.9
$5,000 to under $7,000	9,410,802	321,247	3.4	2.1
$7,000 to under $10,000	12,901,228	105,813	.8	.7
$10,000 and up	23,671,874	39,106	.2	.3

Source: IRS, *Statistics of Income, 1970.*

nontaxable—either to provide equity by adjusting for special burdens or to carry out public policy by providing incentives for certain activities and disincentives for others. As a result, one in every 605 tax returns with an adjusted gross income of $10,000 or over (that is, one-sixth of 1 percent of the total) was nontaxable in 1970.

In conclusion, then, it is a myth that many millionaires and other wealthy persons can and do avoid paying income taxes by escaping through loopholes in the Internal Revenue Code. This claim has been voiced too often, either carelessly or deliberately, and it has succeeded in creating resentment that has led to a "soak the rich" attitude among broad sections of the public and in Congress. The time has come for this myth to be laid to rest. The fact is that many of those taxpayers who submitted returns with a high adjusted gross income did not have a high income. They only *appeared* to have a high income by following the procedural requirements of the income tax form.

This does not mean, of course, that huge amounts of income do not escape taxation or that many taxpayers do not manage in some way or other to avoid bearing their proper share of the overall burden. This problem will be reviewed in the next chapter.

2

Who Gets the Untaxed
Personal Income?

At the outset, the Internal Revenue Code proclaims its intent to tax "all income from whatever source derived." But then it undercuts that sweeping statement by allowing a myriad of exclusions, exemptions, deductions and credits that free about half of all personal income from the impact of the income tax. Over $400 billion remained untaxed in 1970 and the figure was probably in excess of $460 billion for 1972. This makes the federal income tax the tax with the most liberal exemptions—and the narrowest actual base compared with its potential base—in the United States. Sales and property tax exemptions average little more than one-fourth of their overall computed or estimated base.

Table 3

RELATIONSHIP OF PERSONAL INCOME, ADJUSTED GROSS
INCOME AND TAXABLE INCOME ON
FEDERAL INCOME TAX RETURNS, 1950-1970

($ in billions)

Year	Personal Income	Adjusted Gross Income	Taxable Income	AGI as a Percent of PI	Taxable Income as a Percent of AGI	Taxable Income as a Percent of PI
1950	$227.6	$179.9	$ 84.9	79.0%	47.2%	37.4%
1955	310.9	249.4	128.0	80.2	51.3	41.2
1960	401.0	316.6	171.6	78.9	54.2	42.8
1965	538.9	430.7	255.1	79.9	59.2	47.3
1969	750.9	605.6	388.8	80.6	64.2	51.8
1970	806.3	632.0	401.2	78.4	63.5	49.8

Source: IRS, *Statistics of Income, Individual Income Tax Returns,* various years; personal income statistics from the *Economic Report of the President,* January 1973.

Contrary to what is widely believed, the percentage of personal income that is subjected to federal taxation has been gradually increasing over the years, from 37.4 percent in 1950 to a high of 51.8 percent in 1969 (see Table 3). But this progress in making the income tax more comprehensive was not achieved primarily by purposeful tax reform, either by tightening or closing so-called loopholes. Rather, it came about as a result of certain extraneous factors. Growth in incomes and continuous inflation pushed an increasing share of reported income above the personal exemption, which remained steady at $600 from 1948 through 1969; then, personal exemptions were raised for 1970 and again for 1971 and 1972. These higher personal exemptions and other "tax reforms" in the Tax Reform Act of 1969, along with economic trends, helped lower the percentage of personal income subject to the income tax from 51.8 percent in 1969 to 49.8 percent in 1970.

Sources of Untaxed Income

The $405 billion gap between personal income and taxable income in 1970 can be traced to two sources: (1) a $231 billion difference between adjusted gross income and taxable income—a figure that can be derived accurately and in detail from the annual statistics of income tax returns supplied by the Internal Revenue Service; and (2) a $174 billion difference between personal income and adjusted gross income—a figure whose composition can only be estimated. As Table 3 shows, adjusted gross income has remained steady at about 80 percent of personal income over the past 20 years; taxable income as a percentage of adjusted gross income, however, gradually climbed from 47 to 64 percent.

While the difference between personal income and taxable income equals $405 billion, total untaxed income may be estimated at $465 billion because of $60 billion in offsetting items. Major items of untaxed income and offsets are shown in Table 4.

The literature of the tax reform drive usually asserts that most of the "loopholes" were designed for and work to the benefit of the rich, that poor and middle-income taxpayers are taxed on all of their income with no escape possibilities and that most of the income that avoids taxation is to be found in the very high-income brackets. Table 4, however, suggests the opposite: much or most of the untaxed income is in the low- and medium-income brackets.

28

Table 4
MAJOR ITEMS OF FEDERALLY UNTAXED INCOME, 1970
Reconciliation of Personal Income and Taxable Income
on Federal Income Tax Returns
(estimated)

	$ Billions	% of Total PI
Personal income (PI)	806	100.0
Taxable income reported on federal income tax returns (TI)	401	49.8
Federally untaxed personal income (difference between PI and TI)	405	50.2

		% of Federally Untaxed PI
Tax-free income from social benefits		
Social security, unemployment compensation, public assistance, veterans' benefits, et cetera	72	17.8
Untaxed labor income		
Employer contributions to pension and welfare funds, nontaxable income in kind, nontaxable military pay allowances, et cetera	32	7.9
Imputed income		
Rent on owner-occupied homes, earnings on insurance policies, food and fuel produced and consumed on farms, et cetera	45	11.1
Tax-exempt interest on municipal bonds	2	.5
Nonreported income		
Persons with income below taxable level filing no return, amounts disclosed by audit, evasion	46	11.4
Other nontaxed income		
Property income received by nonindividuals (fiduciaries, nonprofit institutions), excluded business expenses, et cetera	20	4.9
Personal exemptions		
$625 for 195 million persons plus 9 million double for aged and blind	128	31.6
Deductions		
Standard deductions	$32	
Itemized deductions:		
State & local taxes	32	
Interest paid	24	
Charitable contributions	13	
Medical expenses	10	
Other	9	
	$88	120	29.6
All nontaxed income		$465	114.8

Table 4 *(continued)*

	$ Billions	% of Total PI
Minus		
Exemptions and deductions in excess of AGI on nontaxable returns:		
Standard deductions	$14	
Itemized deductions	4	
Personal exemptions	21	
	$39	
AGI on those returns	22	−17	−4.2
Taxed income *not* included in personal income as defined in national income accounting:		
Personal contributions for social insurance	$28	
One-half of capital gains	9	
Other	6	−43	−10.6
Difference between PI and TI (as above)	$405	100.0

Source: Derived by author from data in IRS, *Statistics of Income, 1970.*

Tax-free social benefits (such as social security, unemployment compensation and public assistance), untaxed labor income and standard deductions are concentrated in the low brackets. Untaxed income in those categories totals $136 billion. Moreover, one-half of the non-reported income can be attributed to persons with income below taxable levels who file no returns: this must be added for a total of about $160 billion. Personal exemptions and imputed income (imputed rental on owner-occupied homes, et cetera) as well as the remainder of non-reported income are widely, and probably evenly, distributed among taxpayers at all levels and do not gravitate toward the upper income brackets. These benefits total about $200 billion. But even itemized deductions of $88 billion are relatively heavier in the lower brackets (Table 5).

Conclusive evidence on the distribution of the untaxed income by income classes could be obtained by relating personal income to taxable income by income brackets. Unfortunately, however, a breakdown of personal income by income brackets has not been published by the Department of Commerce, nor by anyone else, since 1964 and there

Table 5
ITEMIZED DEDUCTIONS AS A PERCENT OF ADJUSTED GROSS INCOME, 1970

Adjusted Gross Income Bracket	Percent
All returns	19.6
Under $5,000	35.0
$5,000 to under $10,000	23.0
$10,000 to under $15,000	19.1
$15,000 or more	17.4

Source: IRS, *Statistics of Income, 1970.*

Table 6
DIFFERENCE BETWEEN ADJUSTED GROSS INCOME AND TAXABLE INCOME, BY MAJOR INCOME CLASSES, 1970

Adjusted Gross Income Class	Difference between AGI and TI (billions)	Difference as Percent of AGI
All returns	$231	36.5
Under $10,000	114	48.9
$10,000 to $24,999	96	31.1
$25,000 and more	21	22.8

are presently no plans to prepare such statistical information. A detailed comparison between adjusted gross income and taxable income is available from the annual *Statistics of Income* of the Internal Revenue Service and, as Table 6 indicates, it clearly shows that reported untaxed income occurs largely in the lower brackets.

Greater detail by income brackets is shown in Table 7. The figures given there indicate that (1) the major part of the difference between adjusted gross income and taxable income lies in the lower and middle-income brackets—that is, very little is at the top—and (2) effective tax rates on adjusted gross income and on taxable income are steeply progressive. Since most of the difference between personal income and adjusted gross income accrues to persons in the low brackets, the tendency favoring low-income persons is considerably stronger than the table suggests.

The Treasury fiscal staff, under the direction of Assistant Secretary Stanley Surrey, prepared a table in 1968 that incorporated a modified

Table 7

ADJUSTED GROSS INCOME, TAXABLE INCOME AND EFFECTIVE
TAX RATES ON FEDERAL INCOME TAX RETURNS, 1970

Adjusted Gross Income Class	Adjusted Gross Income (billions)	Taxable Income (billions)	Difference between AGI and TI (Untaxed Income) as Percent of Adjusted Gross Income	Effective Tax Rate on	
				AGI	TI
Total	$632.0	$401.0	36.6%	13.8%	20.9%
No AGI	− 2.4	—	—	—	—
Under $5,000	67.6	23.0	66.0	7.7	15.8
$5,000 to under $7,000	56.4	31.1	44.8	9.6	16.8
$7,000 to under $10,000	109.3	65.6	40.0	10.6	17.5
$10,000 to under $15,000	171.9	112.2	34.7	12.0	18.4
$15,000 to under $25,000	136.8	97.6	28.6	14.6	20.4
$25,000 to under $50,000	55.0	42.1	23.5	19.6	25.6
$50,000 to under $100,000	23.1	18.4	20.4	28.9	36.1
$100,000 to under $200,000	8.2	6.4	21.3	37.0	46.9
$200,000 to under $500,000	3.7	2.7	24.9	42.7	56.5
$500,000 to under $1,000,000	1.2	.9	27.9	45.5	62.5
$1,000,000 and more	1.3	.9	29.5	46.5	65.3

Source: IRS, *Statistics of Income, 1970.*

definition of adjusted gross income. However, only a few selected items—one-half of long-term capital gains, exclusions due to percentage depletion and excess of farm losses over farm gains—were added to arrive at "amended adjusted gross income." In other words, the authors included certain untaxed items that they felt ought to be taxable, but did not include most of the large items currently excluded from adjusted gross income. With such selective adjustment, the results are not surprising: effective tax rates for incomes under $20,000 were not affected at all by the "adjustment," but effective rates for the higher brackets were sharply reduced. For incomes of $1,000,000 or more, effective rates dropped from 44.3 to 28.4 percent, for incomes between $500,000 and under $1 million from 44.1 to 30.7 percent.[1] Subsequently such statements about effective rates under "amended" adjusted gross income were widely and repeatedly used to show that high income earners are paying very low tax rates and that their taxes ought to be increased.

Joseph A. Pechman and Benjamin A. Okner used a broader concept of "expanded adjusted gross income" to demonstrate the low level of effective income tax rates. They included a much wider range of items than did Surrey, but again it was mainly a question of which untaxed items the authors thought ought to be taxed. Their results suggested that the effective income tax rate rises from 0.5 percent on incomes under $3,000 to a maximum of 32.1 percent on incomes of $1 million and over.[2] While these figures are less lopsided than Surrey's, it is doubtful that such manipulations truly present an impartial picture.

The fact remains that although public discussion of loopholes and untaxed income has almost exclusively focused on the rich in recent years, most of the untaxed income is in the lower and middle brackets. There are good reasons for this. Under a system of taxing according to taxpaying capacity, persons and families at the lower levels will be largely free of taxation because they need most or all of their resources to sustain themselves at an adequate or minimum standard of living.

---

[1] U.S. Treasury Department, *Tax Reform Studies and Proposals,* joint publication of the Committee on Ways and Means of the U.S. House of Representatives and Committee on Finance of the U.S. Senate (Washington, D.C.: U.S. Government Printing Office, 1969), part 1, p. 81.

[2] Joint Economic Committee Hearings, *Economics of Federal Subsidy Programs,* p. 71.

Redistribution of Income

In 1970 about one-fifth of all individual income tax returns were non-taxable—97 percent of them reporting adjusted gross income under $5,000.[3] Since persons at the lowest income levels generally do not file tax returns, we may estimate that at least one-fourth of the American population paid no federal income tax in 1970. Their number is bound to grow since personal exemptions were boosted to $750 for 1972, standard deductions to 15 percent of adjusted gross income (with a $2,000 maximum) and the low-income allowance to $1,300. A single person with an income less than $2,050, or a couple with two children (or a couple both 65 years or over) with an income less than $4,300, will no longer need to file a return. Additional millions of Americans will thus be freed from any tax liability and more billions of income will become tax exempt.

This may be justified on equity grounds. But it brings about a division of the population—between those who pay the taxes and others, equally entitled to vote, who are interested mainly in obtaining higher benefits from government. In some cases of course there is a clear need for such assistance, but there are also those who will make extravagant demands, knowing that others will pay the cost and that they themselves will not be called upon to foot any part of the bill. If such "representation without taxation" assumes large enough proportions, it invites civic irresponsibility and poses a danger to the preservation of responsible free government. It could lead to demagoguery, to exaggerated promises of more "bread and circuses" by reckless politicians. Not without reason did H. L. Mencken define an election as an advance auction of stolen goods.

To be sure, the drive for greater economic equality, toward raising income in the lowest brackets, has long had broad popular support. On the whole, it has been quite successful—not only during the New Deal and World War II, but also in the postwar period. Table 8, which gives the distribution of families by "money income" class for the three years 1950, 1960 and 1970, shows a decrease in the percentage of families in the lower income classes and an increase in the percentage of families in the middle-income classes. In 1950, 68.6 percent of families had a total money income of less than $7,000 (1970 constant dollars); in 1970 only 31.1 percent were in this category. In just 20 years, income

---

[3] See Table 2, p. 25.

Table 8
DISTRIBUTION OF FAMILIES BY MONEY INCOME,
SELECTED YEARS, 1950-1970
(in 1970 dollars)

Money Income Class	1950	1960	1970
Total	100.0%	100.0%	100.0%
Under $3,000	22.8	15.6	8.9
$3,000 to $4,999	22.1	14.1	10.4
$5,000 to $6,999	23.7	16.7	11.8
$7,000 to $9,999	18.3	24.7	19.9
$10,000 to $14,999	13.2	19.3	26.8
$15,000 and over	13.2	9.5	22.3
Median income	$5,385	$7,376	$9,867

Note: "Money income," the concept by which the Department of Commerce computes income distribution, uses a broader definition of income than adjusted gross income on tax returns. The figures are derived from the Bureau of the Census annual surveys rather than Internal Revenue statistics. In 1970, money income in the United States totalled $577 billion.

Source: Bureau of the Census, *Income in 1970 of Families and Persons in the United States,* Current Population Series P-60, no. 80, 1971.

patterns shifted so that 46.7 percent of families now receive incomes between $7,000 and $15,000.

The question is how much government should, through its tax and expenditure policies, seek to redistribute income toward the lower brackets. That policy, by its very nature, promotes consumption but exerts a dampening effect on capital formation and industrial expansion. It is well established that a high rate of savings and nonresidential (business) investment is associated with high rates of growth. Conversely, disincentives to savings and investment tend to retard economic growth and job creation. While heavy taxation of the rich and of business generally has a powerful political appeal, it exacts a heavy price in slower economic growth and high unemployment. Still, elective officials *cannot* forget that four out of every five income tax returns for 1970 reported adjusted gross income under $13,000 and 94 percent were under $20,000. On the other hand, only 1.8 percent of all tax returns (or 1.3 million) reported adjusted gross income of $30,000 or more, and a mere one-tenth of one percent (78,000) an income of $100,000 or more. That distribution of voting strength inevitably influences considerations of tax policy.

When specific tax changes are under consideration, lawmakers are conscious that 87 percent of all income tax returns are in the under-$15,000 adjusted gross income category—and in that bracket, wages and salaries account for 90 percent of all income, while the aggregate of capital gains, dividends and business profits represents only 5 percent (figures for 1970). On $100,000-and-over returns, however, dividends, capital gains and profits account for 63 percent of all income, wages and salaries for only 25 percent. Understandably, political arithmetic plays a major role in public pronouncements on tax reform and has an impact on floor votes and final decisions.

Does equity mean equality? Though the debate over tax reform deals extensively with economic policy considerations, the movement's "gut issue" is equity in taxation, or more specifically, redistribution of income to provide greater equality in after-tax income. The basic aim of many backers of the present tax reform drive is to shift more income from those who have more to those who have less. As Henry C. Simons, University of Chicago economist, wrote a third of a century ago: "The case for drastic progression in taxation must be rested on the case against inequality—on the ethical or aesthetic judgment that the prevailing distribution of wealth and income reveals a degree (and/or kind) of inequality which is distinctly evil or unlovely." [4] The case for reducing or eliminating income inequality rests in Simons's words on another ethical precept: "At any rate it may be best to start by denying any justification for prevailing inequality in terms of personal desert." [5] The late University of Wisconsin economist Harold M. Groves expressed it plainly: "Many people regard inequalities of income as a clear case of the tyranny of the strong and fortunate over the weak and poorly endowed." [6]

A recent and widely acclaimed work by John Rawls, *A Theory of Justice,* presents other current trends in egalitarian thought. Rawls asserts that a social order is just and legitimate *only* to the degree that it is directed to the redress of inequality:

> There is no more reason to permit the distribution of income and wealth to be settled by the distribution of natural assets than by historical and social fortune. . . . No one deserves his

---

[4] Henry C. Simons, *Personal Income Taxation* (Chicago: University of Chicago Press, 1938), p. 18.
[5] Ibid.
[6] Harold M. Groves, *Financing Government* (New York: Henry Holt & Co., 1946), p. 31.

greater natural capacity, nor merits a more favorable starting place in society. . . . All social primary goods—liberty and opportunity, income and wealth, and the bases of self-respect —are to be distributed equally unless an unequal distribution of any or all these goods is to the advantage of the least favored.[7]

Reviewing Rawls's theory, Daniel Bell called the book "the most comprehensive effort in modern philosophy to justify a socialistic ethic" and added: "It is striking that Rawls, like Jencks, does not discuss either 'work' or 'effort'—as if those who had succeeded, in the university, or in business or government, had done so largely by contingent circumstances or fortune or social background." [8] Some feel that the denial of any merit in economic success is based largely on envy and jealousy.[9] In light of such complex questions, some authors have expressed amazement that egalitarian theories have become so widely accepted and that for some people the issue is no longer even considered controversial.[10]

Some regard redistribution of income from the top down as a clear case of tyranny and exploitation of a productive but vote-weak minority by a greedy and vote-strong majority, and feel that rewards for effort are still necessary. University of Chicago law professors Walter J. Blum and Harry Kalven, Jr., have argued: "Whatever we may think in moments of tranquility, we do not live from day to day without the help of the assumption that those around us and we ourselves deserve in some way the praise and blame, the rewards and the punishments, we all dispense and receive." [11] Blum and Kalven referred to the ever-present danger that tax legislation may be turned into (or is) "class legislation

---

[7] As quoted in Daniel Bell, "On Meritocracy and Equality," *The Public Interest,* Fall 1972, pp. 55 and 56.

[8] Ibid., pp. 57 and 58. Christopher Jencks also attributes economic success to luck or fortuitous circumstances and therefore not a matter of personal merit that would justify a reward in the form of higher income or status. "Economic success seems to depend on varieties of luck and on-the-job competence that are only moderately related to family background, schooling, or scores on standards tests." Christopher Jencks et al., *Inequality: A Reassessment of the Effect of Family and Schooling in America* (New York: Basic Books, 1972), p. 8.

[9] Helmut Schoeck, *Envy: A Theory of Social Behavior* (New York: Harcourt, Brace & World, 1970).

[10] For example, see Irving Kristol, "About Equality," in *Commentary,* November 1972.

[11] Blum and Kalven, *The Uneasy Case for Progressive Taxation* (Chicago: University of Chicago Press, 1953), p. 82.

in its most naked form." [12] In fact, former Senator Joseph S. Clark declared that the "tax issue is at heart a class issue" and may be viewed largely in terms of a "class struggle." [13]

The single-minded concentration of much of the tax reform drive of the past 15 years on the elimination of certain "loopholes" that account for a tiny fraction of untaxed personal income—but which largely benefit high-income persons—and the complete disregard of the overwhelming bulk of untaxed income that redounds to recipients in the lower and middle brackets makes the thrust of the movement primarily to alter, through the political process, the rewards and punishments of the free market system. The question is whether the existing bias against effort and success in our society and in our tax system should be made stronger by a type of tax reform that adds to it or whether neutrality is a more desirable goal of tax reform.

In a sophisticated little book entitled *The Ethics of Redistribution,* Bertrand de Jouvenel pointed at the pitfalls and dangers of increasingly shifting income from those who earn it by producing goods or services for the market to those who do not.[14] He pointed out that a steady whittling down of incentives must lead to a decline in productivity, that it must mean the end of many culturally desirable activities, and that it leads to a steady growth in the power of the state. If taxing at the top does not yield enough, a state will proceed to impose ever heavier taxation on everyone above an income floor.

A new direction? Trends in public sentiment are often hard to appraise. In its fall 1969 issue, *The Public Interest* carried an article by Joseph A. Pechman, "The Rich, the Poor and the Taxes They Pay," strongly advocating a type of tax reform that would redistribute income. Three years later (summer 1972), it featured Irving Kristol's article, "Of Populism and Taxes," which warned that the modern populism of income redistribution by taxation may be losing support among a majority of the American people who are disillusioned with its results and perceive its shortcomings: "One can fairly predict that many middle-class reformers will find, to their surprise, that the populace is going to be quick to bite the hand that aims to feed it. The populace doesn't want

---

[12] Ibid., p. 20.
[13] *Congressional Record,* April 5, 1960, p. A 3008.
[14] Bertrand de Jouvenel, *The Ethics of Redistribution* (New York: Cambridge University Press, 1952).

to be fed: it wants more freedom to graze on its own." [15] Whether Irving Kristol assessed the American public's current mentality correctly or not may become apparent during consideration of income tax reform in 1973.

Library of
Davidson College

3
Deductions, Capital Gains and
Other Tax Benefits

Capital Gains Taxation

Of all the tax "loopholes" none is cited more often as a glaring example of the tax system's unfairness than taxation of long-term capital gains at half the normal income tax rate. In the words of the First National City Bank of New York: "It is seen by some as a nefarious device by which the rich avoid paying very high rates on top-bracket incomes, the Treasury loses billions in revenues, and the progressivity of the income tax is weakened." [1] Ways and Means Committee Chairman Wilbur Mills said in the spring of 1972: "It is pretty hard to justify treating a capital gain differently from ordinary income. I've never felt there is anything more sacrosanct about the profit from the sales of an asset than from the sweat of your brow." [2] The most effective statement, however, and the most often repeated during the 1972 presidential campaign, was Senator McGovern's: "Money made by money should be taxed at the same rate as money made by men."

This principle, taken at face value, is persuasive and hard to refute. Why should a man who bought common stocks and sold them after six months at a $10,000 profit pay less in taxes than a man who earned $10,000 by his daily toil over a year? A dollar made from stock profits will buy no less than a dollar made in wages—so why should capital gains not be taxed as ordinary income? Moreover, special treatment for capital gains injects many complications into the tax system and often

---

[1] First National City Bank of New York, *Monthly Economic Letter,* October 1972.

[2] *Congressional Record,* March 2, 1972, p. H 1721.

has more influence on investment decisions than other factors. The income tax law could be greatly simplified by abolishing special consideration for capital gains. Last but not least, capital gains are heavily concentrated in the top brackets and provide little benefit to persons on the lower rungs of the income ladder. For 1970, 93 percent of all returns reported *no* net gain from the sale of capital assets. About half of all reported gains was on returns with an adjusted gross income of $30,000 and up (less than 2 percent of all returns), four-fifths on returns with $10,000 or more. Net capital gains accounted for only 5 percent of the adjusted gross income of taxpayers in the income bracket under $10,000, but for nearly half in the $50,000-and-up group. The higher an income is, the larger will be the share derived from capital gains. Therefore, if special treatment of long-term capital gains is in fact a "loophole," it is certainly one whose direct benefits mainly aid the rich.

But many observers disagree that taxation of only half of net long-term capital gains truly constitutes a loophole. They regard it, instead, as an essential device to provide greater equity and prevent grave economic damage. In their view, capital gains are really not income and therefore should not be treated as income for tax purposes—although these gains may represent *some* taxpaying capacity. For this reason, most countries do not tax capital gains as income—some do not tax them at all, others at lower rates than income—and most tax them more lightly than does the United States.

It is technically correct to say that half of long-term capital gains is exempt from taxation, but this is simply a method of taxing them at one-half the rates applicable to regular income. It may therefore be more appropriate to say that long-term capital gains are taxed at lower rates than current income because they are not current income. National economic accounting has always excluded capital gains from measures of income because nothing is added to current output if an investor shifts from one type of investment to another, even though he does it at a higher price than the one at which he had bought the asset. But to an individual a capital gain *may* constitute income—certainly by R. M. Haig's classic definition: "Income is the money value of the net accretion to one's economic power between two points in time." [3] That concept, if accepted, would call for taxing a person's consumption, plus the

[3] Robert M. Haig, ed., *The Federal Income Tax* (New York: Columbia University Press, 1921), Chapter 1.

year-to-year change in his net wealth. This, in turn, implies taxing unrealized as well as realized gains, something that is undesirable for a variety of reasons and could be economically destructive.

There are several arguments why even realized gains should not be taxed like ordinary income. Assets held for a number of years, or even for a decade or more, may have increased in price merely because of inflation. Consumer prices have risen 25 percent in the past five years, 40 percent in the past ten, and nearly 100 percent in the last quarter century. To tax such a "gain" would amount to a capital levy, not just a tax on income. Moreover, under a system of progressive tax rates, the bunching in the year of sale of gains that may have accrued over many years could result in an unduly high rate. This problem probably could be solved by an averaging process, just as the inflation factor could be compensated for by an appropriate time adjustment—that is, a rate scale geared to the length of time that the asset had been held. But the basic fact remains that gains from the sale of long-term assets (in contrast to trading gains) do not arise out of current production and are not current income. They merely represent the conversion of an asset from one form into another. Congress has recognized this for homes. It can be argued that there is no reason to treat a "rollover" in other types of investment differently—except the political reason that millions sell their houses for more than they paid for them (or plan or hope to) but only one taxpayer in 14 enjoys other types of capital gains.

As a compromise between the two propositions of taxing long-term capital gains as income and not taxing them at all, Congress resorted to the often applied principle of "splitting the difference" and taxing them at 50 percent of the income tax rate. That compromise seemed to be so widely accepted and to work so well that the principle was extended to activities that only remotely resemble capital gains—coal, oil and iron ore royalties, livestock used for breeding, timber operations, unharvested crops, lump-sum distributions from retirement plans, employee stock options and others. The present system of taxing capital gains at half the normal rate has now been in effect for 30 years and, although certain tightening and other improvements have been made and more may be indicated, this stability suggests a balance of forces that may not be easy to upset.

Capital gains taxed as income? It is widely believed that the income tax law originally taxed capital gains in full at current tax rates and that remedial provisions were not introduced until the Revenue Act of 1921.[4] The fact is, however, that special treatment of capital gains goes back to the Civil War income tax and was part of our present income tax as enacted in 1913.

Subsequent to the first imposition of an income tax in 1862, the commissioner of internal revenue ruled capital gains to be taxable as income. However, Congress countermanded this order by providing in the act of June 30, 1864, that only the profits from the sale of real estate purchased within the year for which the income was estimated were to be taxed, and that the actual losses from the sales of such property might be deducted from the income. Taxation of capital gains was extended (to property transactions within two years, not just a year, of the original purchase) by the act of March 2, 1867. Five years later the Civil War income tax was repealed.

When Congress reimposed an income tax in August 1894, profits from real estate were again to be taxed as income only when the property had been bought within the two preceding years. Soon after, however, the income tax itself was declared to be unconstitutional by the U.S. Supreme Court in the famous case of *Pollock* v. *Farmer's Loan and Trust Company* (157 U.S. 429). After ratification of the Sixteenth Amendment, an income tax was again adopted in 1913. Representative Cordell Hull, who drafted the section of the bill pertaining to capital gains, "evidently intended to exempt capital gains from taxation, but was not absolutely clear on this point." [5] During the floor debate, Hull assured the House that the tax would apply only to purchases and sales of real estate and securities made within the same year.[6] However, the Emergency Revenue Act of September 1916 provided for taxation of capital gains, with asset value as of March 1, 1913, to govern property acquired prior to that date.

---

[4] The Joint Economic Committee staff reported in *The Federal Tax System: Facts and Problems* (Washington, D.C.: U.S. Government Printing Office, 1964), p. 74: "Prior to 1922, capital assets were not explicitly defined in the law. Gains from the sale of all assets were taxable in full as ordinary income both to individuals and to corporations."

[5] Sidney Ratner, *American Taxation* (New York: W. W. Norton Co., 1942), p. 326; J. S. Seidman, *Legislative History of Federal Income Tax Laws* (New York: Prentice-Hall, 1938), pp. 983–1007.

[6] *Congressional Record,* April 26, 1913, p. 513, and May 6, 1913, p. 1257.

Experience with taxing capital gains at regular income tax rates during and after World War I, particularly the resulting "lock-in" effect on investments, led to a movement for change. Secretary of the Treasury Andrew Mellon suggested that it would be sounder taxation policy not to recognize capital gains and losses, arguing that the government probably had lost more revenue by permitting the deduction of capital losses (between 1918 and 1921) than it had realized by including capital gains as income.

Special treatment of capital gains began with the Revenue Act of 1921 which established a maximum rate of 12.5 percent for capital gains—compared with a top income tax rate that was reduced in that act from 73 to 56 percent and in subsequent steps to a low of 24 percent for 1929. Numerous changes were enacted after 1921. Particularly noteworthy is the 1934 scheme of scaling capital gains rates to the length of time that an asset had been held—from 100 percent of the normal rate for assets bought and sold within a year, 80 percent for assets held from one to two years and gradually down to 30 percent for assets held for 10 or more years. The scheme was abandoned four years later because it was held to influence decisions on the length of the holding period. A "sliding scale" of capital gains taxation, geared to the length of the holding period, has an undeniable appeal, however, and such plans are now again under consideration.

Our current method of taxing capital gains was adopted in 1942: 50 percent of assets held for six months or more were subjected to income taxation, with a maximum rate of 25 percent on total gains. In 1963 President Kennedy proposed a reduction in the share of capital gains taxed to 30 percent for holdings of two years or over, but the proposal was not enacted. The 25 percent maximum rate was abolished for gains over $50,000 in 1969, which means that capital gains may be subjected to a rate of up to 35 percent (half of the top income tax rate of 70 percent), and actually even higher because the nontaxed part of capital gains must now be included in the limited tax preferences which are subject to a 10 percent tax from $30,000 on up.

Limited tax preferences (LTPs) may have a greater impact on capital gains taxation than was originally assumed. According to Treasury estimates, the excluded one-half of long-term capital gains may account for more than 80 percent of the total amount of all LTPs, and could exceed 90 percent in 1972. In other words, most of the "minimum tax" on LTPs will be on capital gains. This, on top of the elimination of the "alternative" 25 percent tax rate, may have a disincentive effect on decisions by investors with large unrealized capital gains (and will of course materially boost the tax on those who liquidate their gains). So, at least for some taxpayers, capital gains taxes were effectively raised by the 1969 amendment.

Potential damage to economic growth. For years it has been a prime goal of some tax reformers to subject all capital gains to taxation at normal income tax rates or, at least, come reasonably close to it. The proposal is asserted mainly on equity grounds, but its sponsors also point out that substantial revenue gains—some estimates put them as high as $12 billion a year—may be involved. Most of those estimates, however, assume that a doubling of the tax rate will have no significant impact on transactions or on economic expansion, a proposition that is open to question. Opponents of the proposal argue that the Treasury could even get less revenue because taxpayers might hang on to investments with unrealized profits while liquidating those with losses. In addition, the measure could lead to a slowdown in new investment and in the economic growth rate.

Dan Throop Smith, a tax policy expert who served as deputy to the secretary of the Treasury during the Eisenhower administration, wrote:

> It is hard to imagine any single change in the tax law which would do as much damage to economic development as the full taxation of capital gains, even if the maximum rate were reduced to 50 percent. The risk of loss is so great in so many important areas of investment that anything like a half-and-half sharing with the government would seriously curtail investment. . . . For emphasis it may be repeated that a tax on capital gains is a more serious barrier to investment than the ordinary income tax is to activity because there are no non-pecuniary incentives for investment.[7]

Another observer summarizes the major damages that could result from substantially boosting capital gains taxation as follows:

> First, risk-taking incentives and the supply of essential venture capital would be seriously curtailed.
> Second, investments in modern plant and equipment and in new technologies would diminish.

---

[7] Dan Throop Smith, *Federal Tax Reform* (New York: McGraw-Hill, 1961), p. 146.

And third, the mobility of capital assets—which is crucial to maintaining a dynamic and fluid economy—would be impeded.[8]

For these reasons no industrial nation taxes capital gains as ordinary income and some of the countries with the most rapid economic growth such as Germany and Japan do not tax them at all—in an effort to stimulate capital formation, introduction of new products and methods, and expanded employment.

Some have proposed that long-term capital gains should be exempt from taxation if they constitute merely a "rollover" or a shift from one investment to another. This rule now applies to the sale of a home and subsequent purchase of another residence. Congress realized that no true and taxable gain arises when a person sells his house and buys another one for which he pays at least the same amount. Why should that principle not also be applied to other types of investment? Some have also proposed eased capital gains taxation but these suggestions have not made much progress in the Congress. Others suggest that the tax rate on capital gains should be geared to the length the asset has been held, which was the U.S. practice from 1934 to 1938. Such a plan could and probably should be tried again.

At the present time a short-term gain (held less than six months) is taxed as regular income while a long-term gain (held more than six months) is taxed as a capital gain. It is hard to tell whether this practice is appropriate since there are no hard and fast rules for distinguishing trading gains from investment gains: some more or less arbitrary time period must be established. The question has been raised repeatedly whether the minimum holding time of six months should be lengthened to one year.

Time and again it has been proposed that unrealized capital gains be taxed at the investor's death lest they escape taxation forever. The proposal has never been enacted, partly because it has been a firmly established principle that a gain does not arise until the asset is sold. The more important consideration is the question of liquidity. If unrealized gains were taxable as part of the investor's estate, insufficient cash might be available to pay the tax without a sale. Thus such a tax

---

[8] U.S. Congress, Senate, *Tax Reform Act of 1969,* Hearings before the Committee on Finance (Washington, D.C.: U.S. Government Printing Office, 1969), part 3, p. 1882; testimony by Robert W. Haack, president, New York Stock Exchange.

could force the breakup or liquidation of many family and other enterprises which were unable to raise the necessary cash. If the inheritor were offered the option of assuming the original tax base (purchase price), he could avoid a high tax liability at the same time at which estate taxes (which range up to 77 percent) are also payable. Thereby the forced breakup of the enterprise or investment could be prevented. But the asset might then be solidly frozen in, for years or for generations, because the capital gains tax would become prohibitively high.

The problem would be eased for a period of time by making only the gains accruing after the enactment of the new law subject to tax. But this would produce little revenue gain and would only postpone, not prevent, the described difficulties. In other words, there is no easy way out—contrary to assertions contained in some frequently discussed plans for taxing capital gains more heavily. Consideration of economic consequence and of equity suggests that long-term capital gains be treated differently from income lest serious harm be done.

Mineral Percentage Depletion Allowances

Mineral percentage depletion allowances for individual operators and corporations have long been denounced, to use Senator Thomas J. McIntyre's words, as "the most notorious of the many loopholes now in our tax laws." The senator added that "elimination of the oil depletion allowance is synonymous with tax reform." [9] Senator Paul Douglas, citing his 20-year battle against percentage depletion, called it "the worst abuse of all," [10] and Professor William F. Hellmuth, Jr., who for some time served as deputy assistant secretary of the Treasury for tax policy, told the House Ways and Means Committee that it was "the most glaring and most widely condemned source of erosion in the corporate income tax base." [11]

Oil and gas get a break. Some of the facts are evident: production of oil and gas and of most other minerals from domestic and foreign sources receives certain large tax advantages that are denied to other

---

[9] *Congressional Record,* September 12, 1969, p. S 10490.
[10] *Congressional Record,* May 29, 1968, p. 15741.
[11] U.S. Congress, House of Representatives, Committee on Ways and Means, *Tax Revision Compendium* (Washington, D.C.: U.S. Government Printing Office, 1959), vol. 1, p. 294.

business activities. This has been the case now for well over half a century—with only comparatively minor changes enacted since 1926. Few subjects have been explored, studied, investigated and considered more thoroughly, more extensively, or more frequently by the Congress. At the same time, few public policies have been tried and found so wanting of merit by the news media and by numerous observers, authors and scholars unconnected with the petroleum industry. It is certainly hard to understand or to accept the fact that the owner of an oil or gas well should be able to write off against his profits considerably more than his investment—sometimes several times as much as his actual cost —or why he should be taxed on only half of his net profits. Though the convenience or simplicity of the arrangement compared with prior provisions is obvious, the logic and justification are elusive, to say the least. It is not surprising that percentage depletion allowances and related write-off privileges for exploration and development costs have been the target of bitter attacks from the public and within the Congress year after year for several decades. Yet, such allowances endure, seemingly as solid and rock-like as ever, with only the slight rate reduction enacted in 1969.

When asked about one of the biggest loopholes in our tax laws, Wilbur Mills replied:

> I frankly don't know. Everybody talks about the depletion allowance. But historically the Congress has felt that some degree of preference is necessary if we don't want to be dependent on the production of oil, gas, and other minerals outside the U.S. Some people want to end the preferences altogether, but what would that do to these industries? That's the question. I'd like to see an income tax law where all income is treated alike, regardless of the source. But that's utopia.[12]

Clearly, gas, oil and other mineral producers receive benefits that are not available to other taxpayers. Virtually all other businesses are limited to writing off through depreciation over a period of years only their consumable capital outlays, inadequate as that may be in the face of rapid inflation and the growing intricacy and sophistication—that is, multiplied costs—of plant, equipment and processes. Permissible capital depreciation allowances often result in insufficient fund accumulation for replacement. Percentage depletion, however, means that write-offs

---

[12] *Congressional Record,* March 2, 1972, p. H 1721. Mills, at the time, regarded capital gains as the biggest loophole.

49

may exceed—often by several times—the actual investment in a particular well, or that only half of the net income will be subjected to normal tax rates. Yet most other business activities have also profited from tax benefits in the Internal Revenue Code: benefits more appropriate to the unique needs, demands for incentives, and problems of the operations in question. This applies to everything from banking to savings and loans and insurance, from farming to cooperatives and real estate, from hemisphere trade to small business and education. Oil and gas do not stand alone—though they do seem to be more favored than others.

Whenever and wherever tax law deviates from absolutely equal treatment for all taxpayers, the true dimension of equity is hard to appraise, if it can be determined at all. This is particularly true in the case of oil allowances, since the stereotype of the wildcatter who became a multimillionaire, or of the giant multinational corporation that controls vast fields and markets, tends to hide from sight the large number of operators, small or large, who barely make a go of it or who fall by the wayside. Facts and supposed facts have been poured out by the millions to shape public sentiments. The protagonists' positions tend to rest more on their political philosophies or economic interests than on factual evaluation and detached analysis. To resolve the question of justice in oil and gas taxation as opposed to other economic activities by recourse to objective and impartial data seems an impossible task because the opposing sides of the issue insist on using their own quite different yardsticks. The spokesmen's briefs read like the description of an elephant by the four blind men from Hindustan. It seems likely that a solution will have to be found in a pragmatic approach that focuses more on the probably economic and other *results* of whatever tax policy is adopted, and less on abstract, elusive concepts of what equity might be.

Mountains of statistics have been offered to show that the oil and gas industries pay extraordinarily low taxes and reap inordinate profits, while statistics emanating from the industry have attempted to demonstrate the opposite. According to some sources the Treasury loses between $1.5 and $4 billion or even more a year in revenues from special tax benefits to extractive industries. The result, allegedly, is a severe misallocation of resources and gross overinvestment in gas and oil. In September 1972, Senator William Proxmire presented statistics from the Securities and Exchange Commission which showed that the 18 largest oil companies, with combined profits of over $10 billion, paid only 6.7

percent of 1970 net income in federal income taxes—down from 8 to 9 percent between 1967 and 1969—although the tax rate for corporate income over $25,000 is 48 percent and the average rate paid by all corporations was 36.7 percent. The senator added:

> If the public cry for tax reform means anything, it means that situations like this cannot continue to exist. When companies earning over $10 billion a year pay only 6.7 percent of their actual net income in Federal income taxes and individuals earning just over $10,000 a year who file a joint return have to pay 32 percent, it is clear that our tax code is not equitable.[13]

Representative John B. Anderson, Senator Clifford P. Hansen and others presented a different picture.[14] They showed that most of the reported profits came from overseas operations that had already been subjected to foreign taxes. Combined U.S. and foreign income taxes absorbed 36.5 percent of worldwide net income (up from 24.2 percent in 1968). Moreover, local and state severance and excise taxes tend to be far heavier on extractive industries than on others, aside from substantial property, sales, income and other taxes. It is impossible to unravel here this "numbers game" of who pays the most—or too little—that has been played for so many years. Industries linked in the public eye with big money and powerful lobbies are usually on the losing end of public sympathy. This may have been a factor in the mineral industries' partial legislative loss in the Tax Reform Act of 1969 when percentage depletion rates were reduced. While a full comparison of the overall tax burden on mineral as opposed to other industries would far exceed the scope of this analysis, it appears most likely from available data that at least oil and gas enterprises pay higher state, local, foreign and U.S. taxes in relation to their volume and profits than does business in general. In 1967, according to a study by the national accounting firm of Price, Waterhouse and Company, the 21 top oil companies paid 64 percent of their adjusted gross income in direct taxes.

The proof of the pudding is of course in the eating. If it were true that the after-tax return on investment in oil and gas were much larger than in manufacturing and other industries, as has been claimed, capital —in its eternal search for higher profits—would undoubtedly flow abundantly into those fields. An overcapacity of the product and expanding

---

[13] *Congressional Record,* September 6, 1972, pp. S 14157–14159.
[14] *Congressional Record,* June 26, 1972, p. E 6477, and September 8, 1972, p. S 14367.

reserves would result in downward price pressures through competition, eventually reducing the return on investment in oil and gas.

There seems to be evidence, however, that investment in oil and gas may not be as lucrative as the public image suggests. Gas and oil production in the United States has been increasingly *less* able to take care of existing and prospective needs. Brownouts and blackouts have often had to be imposed and, according to most forecasts, they are not only a possibility for the years ahead but are almost certain to become more frequent. Natural gas companies, unable to meet demands from current customers, have been refusing to take on new customers, industrial or residential; known gas reserves have been dropping sharply for at least five years. Oil consumption has been growing, made possible by greatly expanding imports—presently about one-fourth of U.S. consumption—with the prospect that American dependence on foreign oil will increase to more than one-half of total demand in the 1980s. In light of these shortages and dependence on foreign oil, if investment in natural gas and oil production were highly profitable—yielding a higher return than other investments—it would seem likely that exploration would be undertaken at an ever-increasing pace, and that production would increase and known reserves accumulate. However, the number of oil and gas wells drilled annually has dropped by one-half since the mid-1950s. Would this have taken place if the investment incentives were as great as claimed?

Outlook for energy. Assistant Secretary of the Interior Hollis M. Dole stated at Stanford University in January 1970 that U.S. reserves of gas and oil are being used up faster than they are being replaced. In the early 1950s well over a barrel and a half of oil was found for each barrel taken out of the ground. Now that ratio has dropped below unity for both gas and oil. Thus the ratio between known reserves and consumption has been declining. Yet the demand for energy continues to grow, doubling every 10 to 14 years. Under current projections oil reserves will decline by more than one-fourth between 1970 and 1980 while oil use will jump 60 percent; gas reserves will shrink about 30 percent, while demand will soar more than 50 percent.[15]

Essential demands cannot and will not be met if present policies and trends continue. The United States will depend increasingly on

---

[15] Tilford Gaines, "Economic Report: The Energy Crisis," Manufacturers Hanover Trust Company, June 1972.

imports for its sources of energy, or it will lack the energy it needs to run its industries and meet residential needs. Vastly increased imports could double or triple our negative trade balance, which is now running at a record high level.[16] Moreover, with so much dependence on energy sources beyond U.S. control, the nation's security would also be placed in jeopardy. Three-fourths of the world's known oil reserves lie in the Mideast and Africa, areas that are steadily beset by turmoil and could become inaccessible any time on short notice. Yet, projecting current trends, the United States will depend on the Mideast for half its oil supplies by the mid-1980s or sooner. Imports already make up about one-fourth of U.S. oil needs. This dependence is making the oil exporting countries increasingly aware of their growing bargaining power—a power that potentially could be used to gain a stranglehold on the United States.

Some have recommended a long-term energy strategy of "depleting foreign countries first" while conserving domestic resources for future years. But for American resources to become useful later, their location and extent must be known and that requires a dramatic step-up in the expensive and time-consuming process of exploration and discovery.

All of this means that desirable as it is to give *equal* tax treatment to all industries and all taxpayers, and important as it is that tax equity be real and apparent to all, differential treatment for vital policy reasons may be the lesser of two evils at some times and in some cases. Equity does not always mean equality. Unless Americans are willing to have the government take control of most of the energy-supplying industries, either directly or through subsidy programs—and with them major parts of American industry on a growing scale—there seems to be no alternative to offering sufficient incentives to increased capital flow into gas, oil and some other mineral fields. The United States has become the richest and most powerful country on earth, the most prosperous when measured by the living standards of its citizens, largely because of the ample availability of low-cost energy sources.[17] Energy consumption still is a valid yardstick of economic development and strength. Therefore, the fact that the consumption of energy resources is increasing more rapidly in the United States than the development of new supply has

---

[16] Oil imports alone, at $4 billion a year, account for about two-thirds of our negative trade balance. They could run at $25 billion by 1985.

[17] The United States now accounts for one-third of the world's oil consumption and for over one-half of its natural gas consumption.

broad implications. Eventually a solution will have to be sought from energy sources that are available in practically unlimited supply but are currently not technologically nor economically usable, such as solar or nuclear energy and geothermal power. But for a long time ahead oil and natural gas will of necessity remain the principal sources of energy. There is evidence that, underground and offshore, the United States has ample pools of oil and gas and other energy sources—possibly enough for centuries—but they need to be discovered and developed.

Observers have painted the following picture of energy resource development in the coming years.[18] Between 1955 and 1970, American operators spent a total of $68 billion on efforts to find more petroleum, but it would have taken another $50 billion to have met all needs and maintained a realistic reserve. Meeting needs between 1970 and 1985 will require roughly double the effort of the past 15 years: $140 billion. However, current trends suggest that only $85 billion is likely to be invested. There appears to be no chance of financing an effort of the required magnitude under present conditions. Yet, an adequate future energy supply depends largely on the question of whether 25,000 or 100,000 wells are drilled per year. The U.S. needs to discover more oil and natural gas in the next 15 years than has been found throughout its history. The controlling element, the key to whether this will be done, is availability of sufficient venture capital: such investment must be made more attractive—that is, more profitable—*after* taxes.

Concern about treating gas and oil differently from most other industries is justified. But there are other valid reasons for such a policy: minerals are "wasting assets" that are used up as they are brought from the ground. Exploration is an extremely risky and capital intensive venture. While one in every nine holes drilled may yield oil, only one in every 48 exploratory wells among the thousands drilled in the United States each year is commercially profitable. Unless potential *after-tax* rewards are commensurate with the risk—high enough to lure investors from other attractions—sufficient capital will not be forthcoming. In a homogeneous world market product, "equal treatment" will not generate the exploration and discovery of oil and gas reserves that the United States must have, now and in years to come.

Special treatment for mineral exploration was not provided by Congress in response to the demands of, or for the purpose of aiding, in-

[18] John G. Winger et al., "Outlook for Energy in the United States to 1985," The Chase Manhattan Bank, June 1972, p. 39 ff.

dustrial giants. It started and was continued as a means of encouraging the discovery and production of more sources of energy and other minerals. When the provisions of the original income tax code of 1913 proved inadequate during World War I, depletion allowances based on "discovery value" were authorized in 1918. Because there is no relationship between investment in a particular well and its productive value, the original depletion allowance was based on the well's value estimated within 30 days of discovery. The intent of Congress was to get more entrepreneurs, particularly small operators, into the game.

But discovery value depletion proved administratively unworkable: estimates within 30 days were difficult to make and too far off the mark most of the time, and court calendars became crowded with pending cases. So, in 1926 Congress decided to relate depletion allowances to a reliably determinable factor: value of the current output. As a compromise between the Senate version of allowing a 30 percent write-off and the House's 25 percent, a 27.5 percent depletion allowance was established—which remained in effect for 43 years. An upper limit of 50 percent of net profits was established that in many cases came to be the controlling factor on less profitable wells. Later on over one hundred other minerals were added to the special treatment list, with depletion rates ranging from 5 to 23 percent.

The 27.5 percent allowance, though arrived at by a somewhat less than scientific method, seemed to fill the bill: it helped supply the country with essential sources of energy, but did not lead to surpluses or unnecessarily large reserves or to excessive profits in the gas and oil industries. Though always an inviting political target, it withstood innumerable attacks from more than four decades until in 1969 Congress decided "that even if percentage depletion rates are viewed as a needed stimulant at the present time, they are higher than is needed to achieve the desired beneficial results on reserves." [19] Depletion allowances for oil and gas were reduced to 22 percent, and for many other minerals accordingly— although no proof was offered that exploration had been excessive or even that known reserves were adequate and growing. Now it appears amply evident that prospects for oil and gas discovery and reserves are

[19] U.S. Congress, House of Representatives, Committee on Ways and Means, *Tax Reform Act of 1969*, H.R. 91-413, part 1, p. 137; U.S. Congress, Senate, Committee on Finance, *Tax Reform Act of 1969*, R. 91–552, p. 179: "The Committee agrees with the House that the percentage depletion rate provided for oil and gas wells is higher at the present time than is needed to achieve the desired increase in reserves."

dismal indeed and permit no complacency. If there is misallocation of resources and overinvestment, there seems to be none in the exploration and production of natural gas and oil.

The United States now derives 94 percent of its energy from fossil fuels. As of 1970, gas and oil supplied over three-fourths of the country's energy, coal one-fifth, water power slightly over 3 percent and nuclear energy .3 percent. The use of nuclear energy will undoubtedly expand but various limitations suggest that only 13 percent of national energy needs will be filled by nuclear sources by 1985. Oil and gas are still expected to supply about two-thirds of the nation's energy requirements by 1985 and about 60 percent by the year 2000. In other words, the discovery rate of oil and natural gas reserves will largely determine the adequacy of the U.S. energy supply for the balance of this century and beyond. Generation of nuclear power may grow faster in the 20th century, as may the utilization of solar energy. Oil shale, of which the United States possesses huge quantities, and tar sands have never been used to produce oil because technological and economic problems are far from resolved. While the slight tax encouragement given in the Revenue Act of 1969 was intended to help with these problems, so far it has not led to commercial oil production from oil shale. More substantial incentives may be needed—possibly along with higher prices for competitive products—to make utilization of this potentially huge resource a reality.

Summary. Percentage depletion allowances for oil and natural gas present a dilemma. Equity considerations undoubtedly pose a serious problem. Somehow the fact that certain industries are permitted to write off more on an asset than they have actually invested in it is hard to accept. But if depletion allowances are viewed as a means to an end—an end that is vitally important to this nation and growing more so with each year—then they have proven their value and should be continued in their present or in a modified form. Senator John G. Tower warned in 1971 that "at the present time our exploration investment is minimal and the level of our domestic exploration is at a 28-year low." To provide an adequate stimulant and to help reverse the trend, he proposed an income tax credit "for expenditures made in the exploration and development of new domestic oil and gas reserves." It failed to pass.[20]

---

[20] *Congressional Record,* November 20, 1971, pp. S 19217-23.

In designing better taxation methods for gas, oil and other minerals, emphasis should be placed increasingly, or even exclusively, on encouraging exploration and discovery (so as to multiply *known* reserves), with production and pricing left largely to market forces. Special tax privileges need not be provided for minerals whose discovery and production are not a pressing national need. But there could be, and most likely would be grave consequences for the economy and security of the United States if—as some have repeatedly suggested—depletion allowances for oil, gas and other strategic minerals were further reduced or even eliminated, without offsetting remedial action.

Admittedly, the logic of mineral percentage depletion is elusive and its appropriateness doubtful, to say the least. There is still a need to search for a better way to accomplish the desired ends. Certainly there are abuses that offend our sense of equity in taxation. The justifiable question of why oil and gas (and other minerals) should be granted tax benefits that are not available, at least to an equal extent, to other industries might thus be answered simply: at this point in time, there seems to be no more acceptable method to achieve ends that are essential to the well-being and future of the United States.

Municipal Bond Interest

While arguments over many of the major tax issues are clouded by factual uncertainties, the substantive questions about municipal bonds are, on the whole, clearcut and noncontroversial. It is a case where two principles, both of which are basically sound and widely accepted, conflict with each other. The policy decision hinges on which of the two principles is to be given priority, which should prevail over the other. The two principles are:

1. Persons of equal income and in similar circumstances should incur an equal tax liability. They should not be offered an opportunity to avoid taxation partially or wholly by means of a "shelter" or "loophole."

2. Governments should reciprocally respect each other's actions and immunities. They should not tax each other or each other's instrumentalities ("the power to tax is the power to destroy"), nor adopt policies that may make it more difficult for other governments—at the same level, or a higher or lower level—to carry out their legitimate functions.

The present system of exempting interest from state and local securities from federal income taxation certainly violates the first principle: any person with money can invest his entire capital, or a major part of it, in municipal securities and thereby avoid paying taxes on an income that may total millions of dollars each year. Continued existence of such a tax haven for the rich appears at odds with fundamental precepts of tax justice.

But to repeal the tax exemption, as has long been demanded by one side in this debate, would open the door to one government placing burdens on another. Without compensating measures, it would tighten bond markets and substantially raise the interest costs of state and local governments. Some public works projects might have to be cancelled. Governors, mayors and other state and local officials and their national organizations have long been adamant in opposing any attempt to tax interest on their securities, directly or indirectly, and they have been consistently successful in warding off such efforts. They argue that such immunity "is vital for the preservation of our dual sovereignty which characterizes our system of government." [21] Freedom of individuals and of communities and local governments is held to be indivisible. They further argue that considerations that might favor taxing their bonds "are secondary to the preservation of the sovereignty of our states and the integrity of our local governments. This system simply could not survive if the Federal Government destroys the preferential character of municipal debt or exercises control of local policymaking by the selective taxation of certain categories of municipal bonds." [22]

Mutual immunity? Some hold that it would be unconstitutional to tax interest on municipal bonds. When the United States Supreme Court invalidated the 1894 income tax act in the case of *Pollock* v. *Farmers' Loan & Trust Company,* it based its decision in part on the fact that to tax interest on municipal bonds would amount to an infringement on the power of the states to borrow money. Whether this position was overruled by the Sixteenth Amendment ("to lay and collect taxes on incomes,

---

[21] The subject was thoroughly covered at the 1959 and 1969 tax hearings. House Committee on Ways and Means, *Tax Revision Compendium,* vol. 1 (1959), pp. 679–791; U.S. Congress, House of Representatives, Committee on Ways and Means, *Income Tax Revision* (Washington, D.C.: U.S. Government Printing Office, 1959), pp. 339–402; House Ways and Means Committee Hearings, *Tax Reform, 1969,* part 6, pp. 2185–2354 (the quotation appears on p. 2190).

[22] House Ways and Means Committee Hearings, *Tax Reform, 1969,* p. 2190.

from whatever source derived") is controversial. Certainly, the possibility that municipal bond interest would become taxable under the Sixteenth Amendment played a significant role in the adoption and ratification debate. The pending amendment was attacked in 1910 by New York Governor Charles Evans Hughes (later chief justice of the U.S. Supreme Court) and by many others as permitting taxation of state bonds. They held that "from whatever source derived" meant just what it said, namely, that there was no limitation upon the power to tax. Proponents strongly denied this. Senator William E. Borah declared:

> To construe the proposed Amendment so as to enable us to tax the instrumentalities of the state would do violence to the rules laid down by the Supreme Court for a hundred years, wrench the whole Constitution from its harmonious proportions and destroy the object and purpose for which the whole instrument was framed.[23]

Senators Elihu Root, Joseph W. Bailey and others made equally strong statements to the effect that the amendment did not grant the federal government the power to tax interest from municipal securities. The debate on the constitutionality of taxing interest on municipal bonds has been going on ever since, and associations of city officials have cited numerous court decisions in an effort to prove that their securities' freedom from taxation is firmly anchored in the Constitution.[24]

Following the trend of decisions over the years, however, it does not appear likely that if Congress were to impose such a tax, the Supreme Court would again—as it did in 1895, prior to the Sixteenth Amendment—find it to be unconstitutional. There has been no test because the proponents have so far been unable to prevail upon Congress to pass such legislation. In 1969, when the House adopted three measures that seemed to open the door, at least slightly, state and local officials went to work on the Senate and saw to it that the three provisions were eliminated in the final conference bill. These provisions would have authorized and encouraged state and local governments to issue, at their option, taxable bonds with a federal interest subsidy, would have prorated deductions between taxable and nontaxable income and would have included municipal bond interest in the minimum tax provisions. But the influence of governors, mayors, county commission-

---

[23] *Congressional Record,* February 10, 1910, p. 1698.
[24] House Ways and Means Committee Hearings, *Tax Reform, 1969,* p. 2227 ff.

ers and other officials proved to be superior. Thus the tax exemption of municipal bonds remained unchanged and may be as firm as ever.

Only one minor restriction was enacted in 1968 and that involved industrial development bonds, singled out because of the abuse of issuing such bonds to finance private developments. Even there, some argue that state and local governments have a legitimate interest in aiding chronically poor rural (and urban) areas to expand their economic potential by attracting industrial or commercial development. Tax exemption to finance this development has been said to be simply another form of subsidizing job creation.

To be sure, tax exemption is not a free gift from the federal government to the bondholder: tax-exempt bonds pay a substantially lower interest rate than high-grade corporate bonds. At the close of 1972, high-grade municipal bonds (Standard & Poor's) were yielding about 5.0 percent per annum, while corporate bonds with an Aaa rating (Moody's) were yielding 7.0 percent and those with a Baa rating 8.0 percent. In other words, corporations had to pay a 40 percent higher interest rate on Aaa-rated bonds and a 60 percent higher rate on Baa bonds than well-rated municipalities.[25] This may be viewed as another, and comparatively modest, form of federal aid to state and local governments.

Tax exemption has been called a very inefficient form of aid because the tax savings of the bondholders may total substantially more than the interest savings of state and local governments. It might be much less expensive for the federal treasury to pay state and local governments (or bondholders directly) the difference between the rates they pay on tax-exempt bonds and what they would have to pay on taxable bonds. In the end, state and local governments would be financially no worse off than they are now but the Treasury would have a net savings; most important, a major "loophole" for rich investors would be closed and thereby greater tax equity established.

Such an outcome, however, could be slow in materializing. Whereas it would be possible to remove tax exemption from *future* issues of state

---

[25] Federal taxable bonds were simultaneously traded at prices to yield 5.5 to 6.0 percent or between 10 and 20 percent more than tax-free bonds. This expresses the greater security of federal obligations which partially offsets the tax difference. Comparison of municipal with high-grade corporate bonds may more nearly represent the taxable versus tax-exempt differential.

and local governments, it is hardly conceivable that Congress would do so retroactively, that is, for bonds already sold at lower rates on the promise that their interest would be tax-exempt. Such action would be regarded as a breach of faith that could have trouble surviving in the courts. If only future issues were to be taxable, the changeover would be slow and the revenue effects would become substantial only after the passage of many years.

Tax exemption of bonds has long been a reciprocal practice between federal and state-local governments. It would certainly be improper for the federal government to rescind the tax exemption of municipal bond interest without paying an interest subsidy to state and local governments. Were the federal government to take such a unilateral action, the states would probably attempt to tax the interest of federal bonds, even though they are now prevented from doing so by statute and court decision. If this denial were set aside and the states were to tax federal bond interest, interest rates on new federal securities would rise, at a large cost to the Treasury. Most of the federal debt is short term, while the maturities on state and local securities run, on the average, two to three times longer. Moreover, the federal debt is about two times higher than total state and local debt and federal interest costs are almost four times higher than such state-local costs. Thus there might in the end be a net loss accruing to the U.S. Treasury.

A boon for the wealthy? The high income taxpayer gains the biggest benefit from nontaxation of municipal bond interest. At current interest rates of 5 percent for tax-exempt and 7 percent-plus for corporate bonds, a taxpayer with a marginal rate of 30 percent (taxable income: single $14,000, joint return $20,000) gets a greater after-tax return on 5 percent tax-exempt bonds than on 7 percent taxable bonds. The higher his tax bracket (up to the federal maximum of 70 percent), the better off he is from an income standpoint with tax-exempt securities. This in itself is contrary to generally accepted principles of tax justice. It puts the decision of whether or not to pay an income tax entirely in the hands of the investor and introduces a regressive feature into the system—namely, the higher the investor's income, the greater the benefit he may reap from investing in municipals.

With the financial advantages so evident, particularly for the rich, one would expect municipal bonds to be eagerly sought after by in-

61

vestors. It would stand to reason that wealthy individuals would put much or most of their capital into such bonds. But strangely, this is not the case. If, in fact, tax-exempt bonds were in great demand, their market prices would be high and their interest rates correspondingly low, leaving a large rate differential between taxable and tax-exempt bonds. But it is precisely the low demand for tax-exempt bonds that keeps their interest rates up and reduces the differential. The tax-exempt feature may, indeed, result in more benefits for the bondholder than for the issuing government.

In the 1960s and early 1970s, tax-exempt bonds accounted, on the average, for about one-fourth of all new bonds sold in the market. Their volume was smaller than that of federal bonds and of corporate bonds as well. This is an open market and tax-exempt bonds are available to any buyer who wants them. If demand were strong from investors aiming to take advantage of the "loophole," the interest differential with respect to other bonds would be high, rather than so low as to raise the question of efficiency. Municipals account for only a small share of the investment market. As of 1972 about $170 billion in state and local bonds were outstanding, up from $24 billion in 1950. Alternative investments included: $800 billion in federal and corporate bonds, $300 billion in mutual savings banks and savings and loan associations, $250 billion in time deposits in commercial banks, $400 billion in mortgages, and $250 billion (market value) in stocks traded on registered exchanges. The returns on all of these other assets, which total in excess of $2 trillion, are taxable. State and local bonds offer the only available tax-exempt investment opportunity. Nevertheless, demand for municipal bonds is so small that the break-even point (where after-tax yield on taxable securities equals the yield on tax-exempt ones) is somewhat below a 30 percent marginal income tax rate, given current market prices.

In other words, investors considering the relative advantages and disadvantages of alternative investments do not rate municipal bonds as highly as the sharp critics of this "loophole" usually suggest. The ownership of state and local bonds, by type of investor (individuals, financial institutions, et cetera) or by income bracket is unknown. But a 1966 study by Professor Benjamin Okner for the Michigan Survey Research Center suggested that wealthy persons do not tend to invest heavily in municipals and that few of them hold a substantial or major share of their assets in tax-exempt bonds.[26] In fact, only between one-quarter and one-third of the outstanding tax-exempt bonds are held by individuals, and ownership is not concentrated at the top of the income pyramid. If tax exemption of state and local bonds is indeed a loophole, most investors do not treat it as such or seize on it as an opportunity to minimize their taxes.

In summary, then, opponents of tax exemption of municipal bond interest present a good case for repeal on equity grounds. No one, and least of all a wealthy person, should be enabled by law to escape income taxes. Even if the lower interest rate that municipals pay is regarded as a payment *in lieu* of taxes, the inequity is only reduced, not eliminated. Fairness requires that all types of income be treated alike.

The equity argument loses some of its force, however, since it is evident that wealthy persons have not taken advantage of this escape from taxation to the extent that might be assumed and is widely believed. Moreover, if municipals are taxed, the prospective revenue gains to the U.S. Treasury are not likely to be great: taxes would probably be applied only to future issues, subsidies would be required to compensate states, municipalities, school districts, et cetera, and present holders of municipals are not necessarily concentrated in the upper tax brackets. Moreover, if the immunity of federal securities is ever waived, the states would probably start to tax interest on federal bonds, which would in turn raise the interest cost on those securities. In this event, there could even be a net loss to the Treasury for quite a few years.

So far, state and local governments have strongly opposed change in this area, but recently there have been indications that they would support optional taxable bonds in return for an interest subsidy.[27] A case can be made for not weakening the access of state and local governments to money markets and for letting them handle their own affairs instead of paying them subsidies with conditions attached. Mutual immunity from taxation among governments and noninterference are long established principles that should be disturbed only for compelling reasons. Whether the reasons are compelling enough in this case is in question.

---

[26] Benjamin Okner, *Income Distribution and the Federal Income Tax,* Michigan Government Studies No. 47, Institute of Public Administration (Ann Arbor: University of Michigan, 1966), Appendix A.

[27] See *Proposed Alternatives to Tax-Exempt State and Local Bonds,* Legislative Analysis No. 3 (Washington, D.C.: American Enterprise Institute, 1973).

Personal Deductions

Personal deductions are the second-largest "loophole"—or diminution of income for tax purposes—in our tax system. Only personal exemptions loom larger. For the majority of taxpayers, computing deductions is probably the most time-consuming part of preparing tax returns. Deductions greatly complicate the computing of taxable income, which increases the workload both of the average individual and of the Internal Revenue Service. They are also probably among the most firmly entrenched and, when under attack, most fiercely defended features of our income tax.

In 1970 deductions totalled $120 billion, nearly one-fifth of adjusted gross income. Of this amount, $32 billion was in standard deductions and $88 billion in itemized deductions (see Table 9). In the preceding ten years, the number of returns with itemized deductions rose from 24 to 35 million—from 39 to 48 percent of all returns. The dollar amount of itemized deductions increased 150 percent while adjusted gross income increased only 100 percent.

Deductions in perspective. Although the Internal Revenue Code uses the "gross income" concept for the personal income of individuals—as

Table 9
PERSONAL DEDUCTIONS, 1960 AND 1970
($ in millions)

	1960	1970	Percent Increase
Standard deductions	$13,002	$32,370	149.0
Itemized deductions			
State and local taxes	10,526	32,045	204.4
Interest paid	8,416	23,895	183.9
Charitable contributions	6,750	12,918	91.4
Medical expenses	5,219	10,588	102.9
Other	4,402	8,742	98.6
Total itemized deductions	$35,313	$88,188	+149.7
Total personal deductions	$48,315	$120,558	+149.5

Source: IRS, *Statistics of Income, 1960* and *1970;* figures for standard deductions in 1960 from IRS, *Statistics of Income, Supplemental Report—State and Metropolitan Area Data for Individual Income Tax Returns, 1959, 1960,* and *1961.*

contrasted to business income which is net—it has allowed certain deductions from its inception in 1913. Speaking to a tax symposium in 1957, Dan Throop Smith, then deputy to the secretary of the Treasury and the principal author of the Internal Revenue Code of 1954 (under which we still operate) declared: "Most, if not all, of the allowed deductions are intended to increase the fairness of the tax." [28] Subsequently he wrote: "All of the deductions allowed in computing the taxable income of individuals are designed to give relief to the taxpayers benefiting from them and thereby make the law fairer." [29] C. Harry Kahn of Rutgers University, author of the standard work on the subject, defined two purposes for tax deductions, to provide greater equity and to promote desirable activities. [30]

(1) *Deductions to provide greater equity.* All exemptions and most existing deductions fall into this category. Their purpose is to refine the definition of income so as to come closer to a "net income" concept that expresses true tax-paying capacity. Therefore, deductions reduce the tax base by taking into consideration special burdens borne by the particular taxpayer. For example, of two men with identical gross incomes, one may have more dependents, heavier medical expenses, unusual casualty losses, or greater state and local tax liabilities. So, he is less able to pay federal income tax than the other. Exemptions and deductions are intended to "differentiate between taxpayers whose incomes, though apparently equal, are of different sizes in some relevant sense." [31] They aim to provide greater horizontal equity.

(2) *Deductions to promote desirable activities.* Tax law provides financial incentives to engage in or support activities that are regarded as in the public interest. Some of these activities are of the type that would have to be undertaken and financed by government if they were not provided by voluntary action. The services of hospitals, schools, libraries, museums are in this category. Congress may find that it is less costly to the taxpayer if government offers individuals or organizations

---

[28] "General Policy Problems of Tax Differentials" in *Income Tax Differentials,* Symposium by the Tax Institute (Princeton: Tax Institute, 1958), p. 6. Smith is now a senior research fellow at the Hoover Institution.
[29] Smith, *Federal Tax Reform,* p. 90.
[30] C. Harry Kahn, "Personal Deductions in the Individual Income Tax," in House Committee on Ways and Means, *Tax Revision Compendium,* vol. 1, p. 392ff.; House Committee on Ways and Means, *Income Tax Revision,* pp. 165–68.
[31] C. Harry Kahn, *Personal Deductions in the Federal Income Tax,* National Bureau of Economic Research (Princeton: Princeton University Press, 1960), p. 174.

an incentive to devote their own funds for such purposes rather than having to underwrite the entire cost through taxes. More important, Congress may prefer that certain activities be carried out under private auspices, partially or fully, rather than under direct governmental control or as a governmental monopoly. Greater diversity is often desirable so as to permit the widest range of individual freedom, consistent with the obligations and purposes of government.

Some deductions are allowed for activities that could not be carried on by government. This applies particularly to donations to churches and other religious institutions and organizations. Government could not, under the "no establishment" clause, expend tax-collected funds for such activities. But it is equally clear that government may encourage —and materially aid—such purposes indirectly. In the *Walz* decision, the Supreme Court was emphatic in stating that though government may not spend public funds for religious purposes, it may indirectly aid them by foregoing the collection of taxes that it would otherwise impose.[32]

Deductions—who benefits? It has often been asserted, and is widely believed, that personal deductions offer a tax haven for the rich while giving little relief to persons of lesser means. But the facts indicate otherwise. As was shown above, for 1970, itemized deductions equaled 35 percent of adjusted gross income in the under-$5,000 bracket on *all* returns and gradually declined to 17 percent in the $15,000 and over bracket (see Table 5). If only *taxable* returns are considered, the comparable bracket is $1,000 to under $5,000 and the comparable figure is 27.5 percent (see Table 10). Only in the $100,000-and-up bracket does the deduction percentage go up, mostly because charitable donations are concentrated in the highest income fields. Table 10 shows, by major income classes, the average deduction per taxable return using itemized deductions and itemized deductions as a percent of adjusted gross income.

The extent and growth of personal deductions have been the object of much criticism as major factors in the erosion of the tax base. Numerous suggestions have been advanced over the years to restrict or cut them back sharply or to disallow most or all of them. Such a broadening of the tax base, it is argued, would make it possible to lower tax

---

[32] *Walz* v. *Tax Commission,* 397 U.S. 664 (1970).

Table 10
ITEMIZED DEDUCTIONS ON TAXABLE FEDERAL INCOME TAX RETURNS, BY INCOME CLASS, 1970

Size of Adjusted Gross Income	Adjusted Gross Income	Itemized Deductions	State & Local Taxes	Interest	Charitable Contributions	Medical Expenses	Other Deductions
		Average amounts per return using the type of deduction					
$1,000 to under $5,000	$ 3,908	$ 1,288	$ 377	$ 377	$ 208	$ 467	$ 172
$5,000 to under $7,000	6,028	1,445	448	413	222	389	195
$7,000 to under $10,000	8,547	1,831	605	607	260	355	222
$10,000 to under $15,000	12,302	2,345	859	788	313	334	253
$15,000 to under $25,000	18,435	3,155	1,276	1,022	453	334	337
$25,000 to under $50,000	32,686	5,379	2,311	1,684	866	463	663
$50,000 to under $100,000	65,997	10,948	4,584	3,379	2,189	678	1,498
$100,000 or more	186,050	41,092	13,171	12,000	13,653	1,143	5,726
All taxable returns	13,009	2,471	920	808	386	355	291
		Itemized deductions as a percent of adjusted gross income					
$1,000 to under $5,000		27.5%	8.4%	4.2%	4.4%	7.4%	3.0%
$5,000 to under $7,000		24.0	7.4	5.3	3.4	5.3	2.6
$7,000 to under $10,000		21.4	7.0	6.0	2.9	3.2	2.2
$10,000 to under $15,000		18.9	7.0	5.7	2.5	2.0	1.8
$15,000 to under $25,000		17.1	6.9	4.9	2.4	1.4	1.5
$25,000 to under $50,000		16.5	7.1	4.2	2.6	1.0	1.5
$50,000 to under $100,000		16.6	6.9	4.0	3.3	0.7	1.7
$100,000 or more		22.1	7.1	4.8	7.3	0.4	2.5
All taxable returns		19.0	7.0	5.2	2.8	2.1	1.8

Source: IRS, *Statistics of Income, 1970*.

rates while maintaining the overall yield. But it appears that too many people and too many large economic groups have—or believe they have—a vested interest in certain deductions to permit the drive for cutbacks to get very far. Experience, repeated many times, shows that demands to repeal or restrict established remedial provisions have a chance to succeed—or be seriously considered—only if they benefit small, vote-weak groups that offer easy targets. If a large segment or a majority of taxpayers find the provision useful and apply it on their tax return year after year, which is the case for personal deductions, attempts at reform are stillborn.

On several occasions it has been proposed to establish a floor under itemized deductions. If the purpose of deductions is to give due consideration to special burdens borne by some taxpayers and to compensate for extraordinary expenses that diminish an individual's tax-paying capacity, there is little justification for permitting the deduction of *all* expenditures in a category. All or most taxpayers pay certain amounts of state and local taxes, sustain casualty losses, defray medical bills or make contributions to some worthy cause. Why not permit deduction only if such outlays exceed a certain amount or a specified percentage of income—that is, go beyond a level normally expected for the average taxpayer? The floor concept is now applicable to medical expenses (3 percent of adjusted gross income for total medical expenses, 1 percent for drugs) and to casualty losses (in excess of $100). It would make good sense to extend it to all or most deduction categories. However, whenever proposals to do so have been considered in the House Ways and Means Committee, they have been decisively defeated due to overwhelming opposition from many sides. It is always more popular to liberalize personal deductions than to tighten them and most of the changes since 1913 have been in that direction.

Deductions versus credits. Some feel that the deduction method is a proper way to adjust income for special burdens. For example, to deduct a casualty loss (exceeding $100) from income may be regarded as a refinement of the income concept because such a loss diminishes an individual's taxpaying capacity. But in most cases, because of the combined effect of deductions and the progressivity of our tax schedule, it is doubtful whether deductions are a proper method of adjustment. When a taxpayer in the highest bracket pays $1,000 in interest, for state income taxes or local property taxes, as a contribution to his church or charity, or for medical bills, he can offset $700 of this payment in his federal tax liability so that the *net* cost to him is only $300. But if a man in the lowest bracket expends $1,000 for the same purposes, he reduces his tax liability by only $140 so that the *net* cost to him amounts to $860. That is simply the result of progressive tax rates. Yet, somehow, such an "upside-down subsidy" seems unfair. Moreover, it misses the purpose of giving relief where it is needed the most.

State and local tax systems have long been criticized for being regressive, often more severely than the facts justify. Actually it is mostly the deductibility of state and local taxes on the federal income tax return that makes them highly regressive. Itemized deductions often reduce the progressivity of the income tax. Since a rich man's tax rate is so high, the deductions he may make for medical bills, interest paid or casualty losses are worth more to him than similar deductions are to the poor man. Itemized deductions may be a larger proportion of the adjusted gross income of the poor man and still worth less to him because his tax rate is lower. Donations for educational and charitable purposes are highly concentrated in the top income brackets because they cost so little *after taxes.*

These shortcomings of the deduction method could be corrected by changing to a tax credit system. Under that system, a taxpayer would deduct a uniform percentage of his outlay from his tax liability, not from his tax base. The net cost of $1,000 in state taxes or medical bills or contributions would then be the same for the rich man and for the poor.

Although the use of tax credits has been discussed at various times over the years, Congress has never seriously considered it. Despite drawbacks in the system, the deduction method seems firmly implanted. In order to understand why, it is important to analyze some of the major types of deductions and exemptions in greater detail. Some of them, such as deductions for state and local taxes, interest paid and casualty losses, have been in use from the inception of federal income tax. Others, such as deductions for contributions, medical expenses, child care and several other purposes, were added later.

Deductions for State and Local Taxes

The main justification for allowing a taxpayer to deduct his state and local taxes is that to do otherwise would be to levy a tax on a tax.

To be sure, most states do just that. Only 15 states (three of them with limitations) permit taxpayers to subtract for state income tax purposes their (much larger) federal income tax; the others levy a state income tax on gross (pre-tax) income. The federal practice of allowing deduction of income taxes and most other state and local taxes appears fair because those amounts are, as far as the taxpayer is concerned, merely transitory—they represent fictitious income that is not available to him and that does not increase his taxpaying capacity.[33] If the principle of deductibility were carried to its logical conclusion at the federal level, the federal income tax should be a deductible item for federal income taxes in the year paid. This was in fact part of the 1913 law, but it was repealed after three years because it reduced the progressive nature of the tax. Even deductions, as presently permitted, make the tax system somewhat less progressive, and for that reason suggestions have been made to disallow them. Deductions for taxes, it is held, are a form of subsidy to state and local governments and therefore a tax expenditure. Would it not be preferable to aid or promote desirable activities by direct appropriations instead of giving general fiscal assistance to state and local governments by deductions for taxpayers? This viewpoint, however, never gained much ground in Congress.

Establishment of a tax credit in place of a deduction for state and local taxes does not enjoy widespread support. Some would allow a credit only for state income taxes—not because they are particularly burdensome and justify special relief for the taxpayer, but in order to force the six states that do not now levy an income tax to adopt one and to offer an incentive to the other states to lean more heavily on income taxes by boosting rates. Others have suggested that tax credits be allowed for the residential property tax, which is widely felt to be the most burdensome tax. The present system of permitting deductions for property taxes discriminates against renters who pay for their landlord's property taxes in their rents but get no tax benefits. The suggested "carrythrough" or comparable benefit for renters would be designed to equal the value of property deductions—or, if tax credits were to be authorized, of credits). Renters account for nearly one-third of the population and, on the average or as a group, are economically weaker than homeowners.

---

[33] Taxes on tobacco products, alcoholic beverages, admissions, were deductible prior to 1964, as were auto licenses and driver registration fees.

Others, however, feel that public policy should encourage home ownership in the interests of a stable citizenry and that therefore property tax deductions for homeowners—but not for renters—are justified. Moreover, it is argued that rent includes the tenant's share of property taxes collected from the landlord. In any event, at a time when complaints about the burdens of home ownership (due in part to high mortgage interest and property taxes) have reached a new crescendo, Congress is not likely to increase that burden by withdrawing some of the homeowner tax benefits.

Interest Paid

The original reason for allowing interest to be deducted from income may have been the fact that much borrowing is done for business and investment purposes, that is, to earn income. Hence this cost should be deducted from income. It is technically difficult, however, to distinguish personal interest from such a business interest. A home may be mortgaged to obtain capital to acquire securities or to start or expand a business. With the huge expansion of home ownership in the past 60 years, a large part of the interest paid deduction is due to mortgage interest. Interest on a home mortgage is a personal expense—as residential property taxes are—for consumption of living space. The renter gets no deduction although his rent undoubtedly includes interest on the capital invested.

Just as in the case of residential property taxes, the sentiment in favor of home ownership is strong and is likely to prevent action that would diminish the interest deduction. While many renters regard the interest and tax deductions as inequitable, there is another solution for apartment dwellers: the purchase of cooperative or condominium apartments, which seem to combine some of the tax benefits of home ownership with the convenience of apartment living.

Medical Expenses

Medical and dental deductions were authorized by Congress in 1942 when, to meet the fiscal demands of World War II, the income tax was turned into a mass tax and the number of returns jumped from 7 million in 1939 to 36 million in 1942. By that time the income tax had been in force for 30 years and tax policy had become much more

71

sophisticated than it had been in earlier times. In authorizing the deduction Congress aimed at the hardship element of medical expenses and intended to aid mainly low-income groups. Contemporary reports had indicated that medical outlays of American families averaged slightly over 4 percent of income and that medical bills of that magnitude could be regarded as part of the ordinary cost of living. Therefore, only medical expenses in excess of 5 percent of income were allowed as a deduction for tax purposes. This was reduced to 3 percent in the 1954 Revenue Act, with a separate 1 percent floor for prescription drug expenses. To encourage medical insurance coverage, one-half of such insurance premiums were subsequently exempted from the 3 percent floor. Possibly an even stronger incentive might be advisable to encourage catastrophic medical coverage. On the whole, medical expenses are probably the least controversial deductions. No significant changes should be expected unless national health insurance with universal coverage were to be enacted.

Charitable Contributions

Deductions for donations are of an entirely different nature than all other deductions. They do not aim to compensate for hardships or special burdens that impinge upon the taxpayer, factors wholly or partially beyond his control. Gifts to organizations for religious, educational, medical, welfare, public (governmental), scientific and similar purposes are voluntary and within the donor's discretion.

Congress authorized charitable deductions in 1917 to encourage philanthropy at a time when, during World War I, tax rates were boosted from 7 percent (1913-1915) and 15 percent (1916) to 67 percent in 1917 and finally to 77 percent in 1918. The deduction was limited to 15 percent of income from 1917 to 1952, then raised to 20 percent with an additional 10 percent for contributions to regular educational institutions, hospitals and churches authorized by the Revenue Code of 1954. In 1969 Congress provided, as a general rule, that the limit would be 50 percent of adjusted gross income. But only very few taxpayers donate anywhere near their permissible limit. Itemized deductions for contributions have run at a remarkably steady ratio of 2 percent of *all* adjusted gross income, and close to 3 percent of income on returns with itemized deductions. The latter varied in 1970 only within the narrow range of 2.4 percent to 3.4 percent in the average

72

of tax brackets from $5,000 to $100,000. Only the top bracket, $100,000 income and over, reported contributions as high as 7.2 percent of income.

In other words, boosting the deduction limit from 30 to 50 percent of income meant nothing to most taxpayers and amounted to pushing on a string. It was probably meant to soften the phasing out of the much criticized unlimited charitable deduction, which was previously permitted under certain conditions and affected about 100 taxpayers, most of whom had an income of $1 million or more. If it were desirable to increase incentives for donations and to encourage large numbers of taxpayers in middle and lower brackets to raise their contributions—or to contribute to all—a shift from deductions to tax credits would be the way to do it.

Charitable deductions have long been under severe attack as "tax expenditures" made without the proper direction and control of public authorities. Government, it is said, has delegated to private persons the power to spend, according to their own inclinations, preferences or whims, funds that rightly belong to the public treasury. It has enabled individuals to make allocations inconsistent with national priorities. Such private control over public funds should be ended. In its place, the financial needs of the organizations now eligible to receive deductible charitable gifts should be evaluated by public officials and met through budget appropriations, as are the demands of other functions and services.

These views are strongly opposed by those who feel that government has already expanded too much in recent decades and taken on too many vital decisions that properly belong in the hands of individuals. Such centralization of power in the national government, it is said, undermines personal liberty, home rule and local autonomy and should be diminished, not increased.

Many or most of the nonpublic institutions that are now eligible for charitable donations—such as schools, colleges, hospitals, welfare, scientific and research organizations—could operate under government auspices and with direct appropriations. Whether they *should* become part of the state structure or remain under private control with indirect governmental aid is a question of political philosophy on which the battle lines are tightly drawn. Repeal of the charitable deductions provision, or its amendment to severely limit or reduce donations, would end much if not most of the voluntary activity in the United States.

73

There is one major area in which government could not substitute appropriations for deduction allowances: religion. Under the First Amendment, as interpreted by the U.S. Supreme Court in a chain of decisions, government cannot expend public funds for religious purposes or organizations. Diminution of voluntary giving to churches and related purposes, as a result of a loss of the tax deduction privilege, could deal a mortal blow to much of organized religion in this country. Yet the American tradition has always held that religious activity merits, and needs, benevolent treatment by public authority. There is a long string of testimony on this question—reaching as far back as "Ye Olde Deluder Satan" law of the Massachusetts Bay Colony in 1647 and the Northwest Ordinance of 1787. The latter asserted: "Religion, morality and knowledge being necessary to good government and the happiness of mankind, schools and the means of education shall forever be encouraged." Several Supreme Court decisions within the past half century have touched on this issue, especially the *Pierce* (1925), *Zorach* (1952) and *Walz* (1970) decisions.[34] In the *Walz* case the Court said in regard to tax exemptions benefiting churches: "Few concepts are more deeply embedded in the fabric of our national life, beginning with pre-revolutionary colonial times, than for the government to exercise at the very least this kind of benevolent neutrality toward churches and religious exercises generally. . . ." [35]

The "no establishment of religion" clause has been a complicating factor in proposals for direct aid to educational institutions—many of which are church-connected—and it has caused attention to shift to indirect aid through tax benefits. Deductions for tuition would not offer sufficient help to low-income families but tax credits could. Tuition tax credit plans for higher education passed the U.S. Senate on three occasions but never got by the House Ways and Means Committee. However, a bill authorizing tuition tax credits in nonpublic elementary and secondary schools (H. R. 16141), was approved by that committee late in 1972 and is expected to be considered again in 1973.

Donations of property other than cash have been the subject of intense controversy, particularly for educational institutions. When deductions are being computed, the value of donated property is easy to determine in the case of easily marketable securities but is less certain

---

[34] *Pierce* v. *Society of Sisters*, 268 U.S. 510 (1925); *Zorach* v. *Clauson*, 343 U.S. 306 (1951); *Walz* v. *Tax Commission*, 397 U.S. 664 (1970).
[35] 397 U.S. 676.

for other types of property, particularly for pieces of art and archival material. These donations may be, and at times are, grossly overvalued. Such abuses, however, can be prevented only by strict case-by-case review and enforcement.

Prior to the Tax Reform Act of 1969, the donor generally did not have to pay a capital gains tax for the difference between his acquisition cost (which in some cases is very low) and the current market value which he uses as a deduction. This made some gifts very profitable. However, the act of 1969 reduced the allowable deduction for certain types of contributions—for example, gifts of tangible personal property, such as a work of art, whose use is not related to the purpose or function of the recipient organization. The reduction for an individual contributor is 50 percent of the amount of the appreciation that would have been a long-term capital gain if the property had been sold. In the case of such a gift by a corporation, the reduction is 62.5 percent of the appreciation. But the tax break still remains for many contributions of appreciated property whose sale would result in long-term capital gains to the donor—for example, appreciated stock held for more than six months and donated to a publicly supported institution. Under the new law, appreciation cannot be counted for deduction purposes in the case of gifts of short-term securities.

In the long run, the basic policy position on the tax treatment of charitable contributions hinges—as it does for so many tax policy questions—on the viewer's political philosophy. Those who believe that, in today's world, government must play an increasing role and should extend the scope and intensity of its decision making are likely to be critical of or opposed to tax benefits for charitable donations. Those with a strong belief in widening the range of voluntary action and individual decision making—and in the right of the income earner to his earnings—favor encouraging private action through tax benefits for donations.

4

Personal and Family Tax Benefits

Personal Exemptions and Standard Deductions

Except for taxpayers in the very high income brackets, much or most of the progressivity in the federal income tax derives not from the rate scales, despite their conspicuous progression from 14 to 70 percent, but from personal exemptions and standard deductions. These particular allowances provide the major tax relief for low and middle income persons. Totalling an estimated $160 billion in 1970—almost double the sum of all itemized deductions—standard deductions and personal exemptions accounted for 40 percent of the difference between personal income and taxable income (see Table 4). They are, technically, the biggest single tax "loophole." With a substantial increase in those allowances for 1972, the amount of income that remains untaxed because of personal exemptions and standard deductions is now certain to be far higher.

Personal exemptions: purposes and effects. The purpose of the personal exemption is to free from taxation the irreducible amount which an individual needs for minimum existence costs and which therefore does not constitute taxable capacity.[1] It is obviously impossible to specify a fixed amount that is proper and fair for both a farmworker family in rural Mississippi and a professional family maintaining a very different living standard in a metropolitan center. Nor does it seem politically

---

[1] The argument is persuasive that amounts needed and spent for mere subsistence are not available for taxation purposes. But by the same logic, for example, federal income tax withheld from wages or paid does not constitute taxable capacity. Yet it is included in the federal tax base.

feasible to vary the personal exemption according to geographical, social or economic circumstances. Only for blind or aged persons were the emotional issues involved strong enough to allow a doubling of the personal exemption.

The decision on a nationally uniform personal exemption, therefore, has to be somewhat arbitrary; the amount that will be grossly inadequate under some circumstances may be ample under others. However, because of the graduated tax rates, the monetary value of the current $750 exemption varies from $105 in the lowest income bracket to $525 in the highest. A tax credit would provide more even benefits than an exemption, at all income levels, and several states have adopted such a system. But on a nationwide basis the credit method would raise the question of differential requirements more strongly.

The $3,000 exemption that the 1913 income tax law allowed the individual taxpayer ($4,000 for couples) was reduced to $1,000 in World War I and to a low of $500 in World War II. It was raised to $600 in 1948 and remained there for 21 years until the Tax Reform Act of 1969 boosted personal exemptions by steps, to $750 as of 1972. By historical comparison, the present $750 exemption is quite low. Since 1942, when the exemption was lowered to $500 to meet World War II fiscal needs, consumer prices have risen by 130 percent, wages and income by well over 300 percent, and the exemption by only 50 percent. On a maintained "price" basis the exemption should now be about $1,150, on a "wage" basis close to $2,000. This has not been done and cannot be done for a simple reason: boosts in the personal exemption are the most expensive type of revision in the income tax. With 204 million exemptions claimed in 1970, the cost of a $100 raise in the amount allowed per person reduces revenue by well over $4 billion. An increase to a level that is economically comparable to the one that prevailed in 1942 could wipe out one-third to one-half of all income tax collections. This brings home two facts: the federal income tax burden is now much more severe than it was during World War II and present yields can be obtained only if the tax base is kept broad (that is, the exemption relatively low) because there is not enough income at higher levels to make up for a substantial raise in the exemption.

Standard deductions: purposes and effects. Standard deductions were introduced in 1944 not to provide for greater equity—they did not then and still do not—but for reasons of administrative simplification. When the number of tax returns multiplied about six times in World War II and the income tax became more of a mass tax, it was necessary to reduce its complexity for the vast majority of taxpayers who were not used to dealing with the intricacies of income tax returns. It was also necessary to ease the burden of audits and enforcement. In 1944 when taxpayers were first allowed to deduct 10 percent of their adjusted gross income (up to a maximum of $1,000) in lieu of itemizing deductions, 82 percent of them availed themselves of this opportunity. But as the amounts eligible and reported for tax deductions multiplied after World War II, itemizing became increasingly popular until by 1960, 40 percent of all returns and by 1970, 48 percent showed itemized deductions. Obviously, the simplification value of standard deductions had been grossly reduced as a growing number of taxpayers—now more income-tax wise than their parents were in 1944—found it worthwhile to shift to itemizing.

The Tax Reform Act of 1969 lifted standard deductions in steps to 15 percent of adjusted gross income (with a $2,000 maximum) by 1972. This is expected to cause 70 to 75 percent of all taxpayers, as many as 11 million in all, to shift to standard deductions. The increased use of standard deductions may not necessarily ease tax calculations for millions of taxpayers who in preparing their returns will still want to add their deductible items to make certain that they will do as well or better with the standard deduction. But it will ease the workload for the Internal Revenue Service computers and auditors.

Whether these changes will make the income tax fairer is another question. A major purpose of itemized deductions is to grant relief for such special burdens as heavy medical expenses, casualty losses and taxes. More generous standard deductions inevitably reduce that type of relief. They will also weaken the incentive for charitable contributions. It could be that many persons who used to donate regularly, because the gifts were deductible, may now claim the standard deductions and refrain from philanthropic giving. That could hurt many meritorious activities, a potent argument against raising standard deductions even higher, as has been suggested by some. At this point it is likely that the 1969 changes, which became fully effective in 1972, will be given a tryout for some years until their results can be studied.

At the time of the passage of the Economic Opportunity Act of 1964 (the war on poverty), Congress noted that many persons and families whom the poverty yardsticks classified as poor nevertheless incurred income tax liabilities. It did not seem to make sense to devise extensive financial support schemes for such persons—and then to tax them. Congress authorized a minimum standard deduction of $300 for a taxpayer and $100 for each dependent which freed about 1.5 million people of any income tax liability. By the end of the 1960s, however, due to continued inflation and higher poverty yardsticks, millions of persons below the official poverty level had to pay income taxes. In the Tax Reform Act of 1969 Congress boosted the low-income allowance gradually to $1,300 per taxpayer in 1972. This relieved more than 5 million persons from any income tax liability, and reduced the tax of over 7 million others. While it may seem a matter of equity to free growing numbers of low-income persons from the burdens of taxation, it also increases the incidence of "representation without taxation." It multiplies the number of citizens who vote but bear no responsibility for paying for enlarged governmental services and benefits. As was pointed out above, this poses a danger to the preservation of *responsible* free government.

Split Income versus the Single Taxpayer

From inception it was the intent of the income tax law that taxpayer units with the same income should pay the same tax. For the past quarter century, however, the law has made a sharp distinction between taxpayers who are single and those who are married. Through the use of a joint return and the application of a different rate schedule, a married couple incurs a much lower tax liability on the same income than a single person. From 1948 on, when the "split income" provision was first enacted, single persons paid up to 42 percent more than married persons with equal income. When Congress in the Tax Reform Act of 1969 limited the singles' tax disadvantage to 20 percent, a reverse situation emerged, unintentionally, for some upper-middle income couples and it still exists: if the income of the two spouses is approximately equal they may incur a tax liability that is up to 19 percent higher than it would be if they were not married and each reported his own income. In other words, as the law stands, it imposes upon most unmarried taxpayers a penalty for being single but levies on *some* married taxpayers a penalty for being married. That does not make much sense, and it violates the principle that the tax law should be neutral.

Single persons and their organizations have long been loudly protesting to Congress against this discrimination in the tax law. Within the past three years certain married persons have been complaining with at least equal vigor that they are being fined for being married. Both groups have a good point. But there does not seem to be a simple solution that is perfectly fair to all parties under all circumstances. The present law is the result of a compromise, but whether it is the fairest compromise possible is a matter on which opinions differ. After holding hearings in the spring of 1972, the Ways and Means Committee decided to leave matters as they are. This, of course, satisfied neither side.

For 35 years, from 1913 to 1947, the law contained only one tax rate schedule to which all taxpayers were subjected, whether single or married. Two developments brought a change in 1948. A 1942 law permitted a divorced man to deduct alimony from his income for tax purposes, and it taxed that alimony to the recipient wife. That appeared fair enough, but the result was a reduction in the combined income tax of couples who underwent divorce. For example, under the progressive rate scale, two persons with $10,000 and $6,000 in income, respectively, pay a lower tax than one person with a $16,000 income. To some lawmakers and others that seemed like a reward for divorce and thereby a penalty on marriage.

But what led to congressional action was the problem caused by the existence of community property laws in eight states from California to Louisiana. These laws, which derived from Spanish and French law rather than from English common law, gave each spouse a vested claim to one-half of each other's earnings. This means that in those states the husband and the wife could (and still can) each report for federal tax purposes one-half of their combined (community) income. In the remaining states no such "income splitting" was possible prior to 1948. In a common law state, a husband with a taxable income of $44,000 (and his wife earning nothing) had to report and pay tax on $44,000; in a community property state, under otherwise identical circumstances, he and his wife could each report an income of $22,000 which meant a substantially lower tax liability. The Internal Revenue Service objected to such income splitting by residents of community property states but was overruled by the U.S. Supreme Court which held that the husband could not be taxed on the one-half of his earnings that, under the laws of his state of residence, belonged to his wife.

81

The unfairness of a federal income tax imposed at higher rates in some states than in others was obvious. Nor is it surprising that a growing number of common law states became concerned over the fact that many of their residents paid heavier taxes than the residents of community property states. Some states began to convert from common law to community property law. But this was an extremely complicated process which caused innumerable legal problems and threatened to tie up legislatures and courts for many years.

Congress finally relented. In 1948 it authorized joint tax returns that were subject to a rate schedule designed to produce the same result as if each of the spouses had earned and reported half of their combined income. This restored federal tax uniformity throughout the United States. But it made the unmarried status very expensive, taxwise, for a person in the middle and upper-middle income brackets. An individual could reduce his or her income tax liability very substantially just by getting married. A single person had to pay, between 1948 and 1969, up to 42 percent more in income tax than a married couple with the same income. In 1951 Congress added another category of taxpayer, unmarried heads of household, on which it conferred about half the advantage of a joint return. But this status was and is available only to persons having dependents, not to singles living alone or with other singles.

Single persons were at a substantial disadvantage from 1948 on and continued to petition their representatives in Congress for redress. But being a distinct minority, their influence was limited. In 1970, 42.4 million joint returns were submitted, suggesting 85 million potential voters, whereas only 25.7 million returns were filed by single persons.[2] In 1969 single persons were able to convince Congress that they were being unfairly punished: their tax disadvantage was cut in half, that is, reduced to a maximum of 20 percent over married persons. That may seem a reasonable compromise but, as was indicated above, there are complications, and now both sides are complaining about inequities. Single persons claim there is no reason why they should pay a 20 percent higher income tax than they would if they were married. Working couples with approximately equal incomes in upper-middle income

---

[2] There also were 2.4 million separate returns of married persons (many of them from community property states or in status of separation prior to a divorce decree becoming final) and 3.6 million unmarried heads of households.

brackets believe that they should not have to pay up to 19 percent more in taxes than if they were unmarried.

Table 11 compares the tax liability at selected income levels for single persons and for married couples with only one earner. The one earner situation applied to 55 percent of joint returns in 1970. On another 25 percent of joint returns, one spouse earned 70 percent or more of the combined incomes—which still gives some advantage to couples filing joint returns.

On only 11 percent of all joint returns did one spouse earn between 31 and 40 percent of combined earnings and on only 10 percent between 41 and 50 percent. It is married persons in the latter group—where earnings are approximately equal—who are at a disadvantage compared to single persons. As Table 12 shows, there is no difference at low-income levels, and only a relatively small one at medium-low and top levels, but two persons with medium-high *equal* income pay a tax that is as much as 19 percent lower if they are single than if they are married. This has been called a "tax on marriage," a "detriment to matrimony" and "savings from living in sin." It is unjust and highly undesirable as a matter of public policy.

To be sure, only a small number of taxpayers—couples in upper-middle income brackets with each spouse having approximately the same income—is at a substantial tax disadvantage because of being married. Nevertheless, the law has created an awkward situation and

---

Table 11
FEDERAL INCOME TAX LIABILITY AT SELECTED INCOME LEVELS
ON SINGLE RETURNS AND ON JOINT RETURNS
WITH ONE EARNER, 1972

Taxable Income (after exemptions & deductions)	Tax Liability		Singles' Tax Higher Than Joint	
	Single returns	Joint returns	Dollars	Percent
$ 8,000	$ 1,590	$ 1,380	+ $ 210	+ 15.2
14,000	3,210	2,760	+ 450	+ 16.3
20,000	5,230	4,380	+ 850	+ 19.4
32,000	10,290	8,660	+ 1,630	+ 18.8
44,000	16,590	14,060	+ 2,530	+ 18.0
100,000	53,090	45,180	+ 7,910	+ 17.5

Source: Computed by author from the relevant provisions of the Internal Revenue Code.

Table 12

FEDERAL INCOME TAX LIABILITY AT SELECTED INCOME LEVELS ON SINGLE RETURNS AND ON JOINT RETURNS, WITH SPOUSES' EARNINGS EQUAL, 1972

Taxable Income (after exemptions & deductions)		Tax Liability			Joint Higher Than Two Single Returns	
		Single return	Two single returns	Joint return (at double income level)	Dollars	Percent
$ 4,000 (joint $ 8,000)		$ 690	$ 1,380	$ 1,380	+ $ 0	+ —
8,000 (joint 16,000)		1,590	3,180	3,260	+ 80	+ 2.5
14,000 (joint 28,000)		3,210	6,420	7,100	+ 680	+ 11.0
20,000 (joint 40,000)		5,230	10,460	12,140	+ 1,680	+ 16.1
32,000 (joint 64,000)		10,290	20,580	24,420	+ 3,840	+ 18.7
44,000 (joint 88,000)		16,590	33,180	37,980	+ 4,800	+ 14.5
100,000 (joint 200,000)		53,090	106,180	110,980	+ 4,800	+ 4.5

Source: Ibid.

proposals have been made to correct it. One bill sponsored by Senator Charles Mathias proposes that no couple should incur a higher tax liability than it would if the two spouses were not married.[3]

Simultaneously, a strong drive is underway to reduce or eliminate the remaining disadvantage of single persons. An amendment by Senator Robert Packwood would abolish the tax rate scales for single returns and heads of households and restore conditions very similar to those existing prior to 1948—one tax rate schedule applying to all taxpayers whether married or single. However, to avoid an inequity between residents of community property states and common law states, this proposal would use a different rate schedule applicable only to married persons filing single returns (which would mostly be residents of community property states).[4] The Packwood amendment lost 41 to 55 in 1971 but, on resubmission, was passed by the Senate (by voice vote) in 1972.[5] It was dropped when the bill (on the debt limit, H.R. 16810) went to conference with the House.

The question of the tax disadvantages of single persons—or of married persons under certain circumstances—remains unresolved and will probably continue to plague the tax-writing committees of Congress. On the one side, it is argued that conferring certain tax benefits on married status is an acceptable way to promote family stability and ease the added costs occasioned by family living.[6] Established tax deductions for mortgage interest and residential property taxes, it is said, are justified as deliberate aid to home ownership and family status. Public policy in favor of the family should be expressed through a split income tax rate schedule as well as through the allowance of deductions. On the other side, singles' organizations hold that no person should be penalized for being unmarried, whether by choice or by necessity, and that the tax law should treat all persons alike, regardless of their family status. The reversal in the vote on the Packwood amendment between 1971 and 1972 seems to suggest a shift in congressional sentiment in favor of the singles' viewpoint.

---

[3] S. 3629, *Congressional Record,* May 18, 1972, p. S 8078.

[4] Similar bills were introduced by Senator Ribicoff, Conn. (S. 869), Rep. Koch, N.Y. (H.R. 850, H.R. 14193) in the 92nd Congress, co-sponsored by over 100 other members.

[5] *Congressional Record,* October 13, 1972, p. S 18100.

[6] Others however, suggest that there are substantial economies in family living versus single living (two can live more cheaply together than separately).

5

Summary

The Internal Revenue Code is full of enough exemptions, exclusions, deductions and credits to make a mockery of the view that it should tax all income from whatever source derived. It is no secret that huge amounts of income escape bearing their share of the federal income tax burden. But not too many people realize that that tax now reaches only about *half* of all personal income in the United States; the other half remains untaxed. This makes the federal income tax by far the "leakiest" of U.S. taxes—the one with the smallest actual base compared with its potential. In contrast, exemptions from sales and property taxes generally amount to no more than one-fourth to one-third of their respective bases.

An estimated $465 billion of personal income remained federally untaxed in 1970 and the total may have exceeded $500 billion in 1972. Why does the tax law allow half of all personal income to go free? Surely this could not have come about by mere accident or oversight. According to repeated and widely believed charges, special interest lobbyists have either bribed or fooled congressmen into writing huge loopholes into the tax code, into establishing tax shelters so that wealthy persons can avoid paying their share of taxes or even paying any taxes at all. But the conspiracy theory of tax policy is refuted by the record. No public laws are subject to more painstaking and detailed congressional study, to more extensive open hearings, to more thorough debate, year after year, than the tax laws. With but few exceptions, remedial tax provisions were put in the law not out of inadvertence, ignorance or, as a rule, a desire to give favored groups improper advantages or privileges. On the contrary, most remedial provisions aim to provide greater equity among various economic groups and individuals or to offer incentives for activities that are held to be desirable as a matter of public policy. If Congress retains provisions that have been long assailed as loopholes by some groups, it does so not from lack of knowledge or in response to sinister influences but because its majority believes, after due consideration, that the provisions have merit. In recent years, whenever Congress has considered proposals for tax reform, it has usually widened more loopholes than it has tightened and has wound up with an increase in the nontaxable portion of income—and an even more complicated tax law.

On its face, it would make great sense to switch to a comprehensive tax base, to tax *all* income at half the present rates rather than *half* of it at rates that are twice as high. A flat rate of 10 percent on all personal income would yield about as much revenue as the present 14 to 70 percent rate schedule produces on half of personal income. Moreover, most of the complications in the tax law that make compliance a severe burden on taxpayers and administrators result from remedial provisions (and limitations thereon) and from differential rates and treatment. The income tax could be quite simple and easy to comply with if it were levied at a flat 10 percent on all income—or even on a graduated schedule—provided there were no deductions, exemptions, exclusions or credits. But such simplification runs into big roadblocks.

A telling example of the difficulties confronting framers of tax law is the issue of the married versus the single taxpayer. Single persons used to have to pay up to 42 percent higher taxes than married persons with the same income. In 1969 Congress reduced the singles' disadvantage to 20 percent. But now, as an unintended consequence, there are certain circumstances in which some married couples must pay up to 19 percent more than they would if they were single (whether living together or not). And every possible solution to this dilemma is highly controversial, fought by one side to the issue or by both.

As a result of the 1969 change, there are now four different rate schedules in the law—and many unhappy taxpayers. The best answer might yet be to revert to only one rate schedule for all taxpayers, married or single (as was the case until 1948), and—in order to take care of the special situation posed by the eight community property states—require all married persons filing single returns to use a special scale. Needless to say, even this solution would not make everybody happy. But it would be more equitable than the present system.

Two persons or two families with the same income do not necessarily have the same taxpaying capacity—if their other circumstances or burdens differ widely. Nor are all types of income-producing activities able to bear the same burden in as diversified and internationally dependent an economy as ours. The law must take an infinite variety of conditions and situations into account. Most students of taxation acknowledge that there must be some differentiation, some remedial provisions, and that the idea of taxing *all* income alike, though appealing, is impractical. Realistically, the question is not whether there should be loopholes but which loopholes and for whose benefit.

The most frequent assertion in the drive to close tax loopholes—or for a more comprehensive tax base—is the claim that most existing loopholes benefit the very rich while the great majority of taxpayers in the middle-income ranges, whose income tax is withheld from their wages, have no tax shelters and are forced to bear the full brunt of the income tax. Allegedly many millionaires pay no income tax and others very little. This is the charge that transformed the campaign for loophole-closing into a tax reform movement.

But the charge does not stand the test of critical analysis. Most of the $465 billion of personal income that was untaxed in 1970 redounded to persons in lower and middle-income brackets. Only a small percentage of it was accounted for by the more frequently cited loopholes that benefit directly persons at high income levels.

The biggest "loopholes" are the personal exemption (raised from $600 in 1969 to $750 in 1972) and the standard deduction (raised from 10 percent with a $1,000 maximum in 1969 to 15 percent with a $2,000 maximum in 1972). In 1970 these two loopholes exempted about $160 billion of income from taxation. Tax-free income from social benefits (social security, welfare, veterans' benefits, et cetera) and labor income (for example, employer pension contributions) totalled another $104 billion. Itemized deductions—for state and local taxes, interest paid, medical expenses, charitable contributions, et cetera—amounted to $88 billion. Analysis shows that the percentage of income that is subject to the federal income tax rises sharply with income and that it is highest at top income levels.

Recent tax legislation, particularly the Tax Reform Act of 1969, has freed millions of persons in the lower income brackets of any tax liability, and sharply reduced the taxes of millions more. The resulting situation may serve a good social purpose but it also raises the danger of increased "representation without taxation"—of growing numbers of citizens that benefit from government programs but do not have to foot any visible part of the bill. Voters in this group are likely to clamor for or support ever rising government spending at other people's expense.

The oft-cited tax provisions on capital gains, mineral percentage depletion, municipal bond interest, and so forth, account for only a small amount of lost revenue. More importantly, they were enacted and are retained not for the purpose of benefiting the rich but to prevent serious harm to the American economy. Taxing capital gains as if they were regular income, making no allowance for the special circumstances of mineral discovery and production, tightening up on depreciation, repealing the investment credit—such measures could have grave consequences for economic growth, employment, and the balance of payments.

Steady vigilance and periodical tightening up is necessary to prevent abuses and to block new ways of "getting around the law." But such review is different from wholesale repeal or diminution of needed tax mitigation.

As it is, the American tax structure—it would be ironic to call it a system—is strongly biased in favor of consumption and against capital formation and investment. The American people are paying a price for it. The United States leans more heavily on progressive income taxes than other countries, deals more harshly with capital gains and depreciation than most European nations and is unique in not levying a broad consumption tax as a major producer of national government revenue.

The underlying conflict in the tax reform debate is probably not so much one of economic theory as of ideological preference for greater income equality. Some view government largely as a huge machine for redistributing income from those who have more to those who have less. Others believe that free market forces are the most effective means of stimulating economic expansion, from which in the end all or most segments of society will benefit. It comes down to the old question of whether it is better to fight over how to slice the pie—or bake a bigger pie.

If the battle over tax reform in the past ten to fifteen years is any guide, it appears that there is no grand solution, no simple way to improve the tax system by closing the most often criticized "loopholes." This has been suggested time and again, in vain. The present distribution of tax burdens and benefits appears to reflect, by and large, the balance of power and economic interests among the American people as represented in the Congress. The repeated defeat of plans to close all "loopholes for the rich" while leaving intact other remedial provisions that account for most of the presently untaxed income suggests the existence of a broad consensus and an understanding of the grave damage that precipitate action might cause.

To be sure, there are many shortcomings in the tax law that need study and improvement, with a view to moving in the direction of a more comprehensive tax base. But the answer is far more complicated than most spokesmen for loophole-closing claim. That huge budget deficits can be met and enlarged federal spending financed through the closing of loopholes is not a possibility but a mirage. The realistic and practicable way of ending budgetary deficits is through tighter control of expenditures than we have so far seen.